Illuminating the North:

Proceedings from the Nordic Research Network Conference 2013

eds. Agnes Broomé, Pei-Sze Chow, Nichola Smalley,
Louisa Taylor, Essi Viitanen

Norvik Press
2014

© 2014 Agnes Broomé, Pei-Sze Chow, Harriet Jean Evans, Ian Giles, Adam Grimshaw, Björn Nordgren, Nicholas Prindiville, Victoria Ralph, Keith Ruiter, Louisa Taylor, Barbara Tesio, Essi Viitanen.

Norvik Press Series C: Student Writing no. 2

A catalogue record for this book is available from the British Library.

ISBN: 978-1-909408-16-6

Norvik Press gratefully acknowledges the generous support of UCL Enterprise Knowledge Transfer Champions scheme towards the publication of this book.

Norvik Press
Department of Scandinavian Studies
University College London
Gower Street
London WC1E 6BT
United Kingdom
Website: www.norvikpress.com
E-mail address: norvik.press@ucl.ac.uk

Managing editors: Sarah Death, Helena Forsås-Scott, Janet Garton, C. Claire Thomson.

Cover image: Tuukka Ervasti/imagebank.sweden.se
Cover design: Essi Viitanen, Marita Fraser
Layout: Marita Fraser

This book was produced using Booktype from Sourcefabric. Special thanks to Adam Hyde and Johannes Wilm from Sourcefabric for their generous support and assistance.

Contents

Introduction ... 5

Biographies ... 9

IMAGE AND ARTEFACT

The Many Guises of the Book – Genre and Paratext in the Works of Liza Marklund ... 13
Agnes Broomé

Under the Scaffolding: Cinematic Representations of High-rise Buildings in Tapiola and Malmö ... 29
Pei-Sze Chow and Essi Viitanen

The Horse and his Hero: A Symbiotic Relationship in Old Norse Literature ... 45
Harriet Jean Evans

METHODS AND SOURCES

Anthony Knipe: A Case Study of English Experience in Seventeenth Century Scandinavia ... 61
Adam Grimshaw

Chancellor Oxenstierna's War 1635-1643: A Guide to Archival Sources ... 75
Björn Nordgren

CONFLICT IN SOCIETY

Finnish National Identity and the Ingrian Right to 87
Return Law: A Critical Discourse Analysis

Nicholas Prindiville

Granting Grið, Mercy and Peace: The Treatment 103
of Opponents in War in Eleventh to Thirteenth
Century Norway and Denmark

Louisa Taylor

Visibility, Authority, and Execution in Heimskringla 119

Keith Ruiter

Landscapes of War and Vistas of Peace in 'Margareta 133
Fredkulla' by Selma Lagerlöf

Victoria Ralph

AUTHOR AND SELF-IMAGE

The Fårö Documents: The Political or Regionalised 147
Ingmar Bergman?

Ian Giles

The Art of Entertaining a Nation under Nazi 159
Occupation: Pierre Andrézel and Gengældelsens Veje

Barbara Tesio

Introduction

The Nordic Research Network (NRN) began as a forum for UK-based early career researchers to share their work with peers in a convivial intellectual environment. As a multi-disciplinary gathering, the annual conference provides an opportunity for scholars in all areas of Nordic research to keep up with the diverse subjects and projects being pursued by colleagues across the country. The third conference was attended by researchers from a range of British institutions and took place over two days on the 5th and 6th of September 2013.

Each year since its inauguration, the NRN conference has grown and evolved; this marks the first time the conference proceedings have been published. The conference has provided many new scholars with their first opportunity to introduce their research to the academic community. This book, similarly, gives a number of early career researchers a chance to see their work in print and reach a wider audience.

By publishing the conference proceedings, we also wanted to introduce postgraduates to the book publishing process by involving them in the writing, reviewing, and editing of a concrete product, providing a rare opportunity to gain first-hand experience of producing a volume from start to finish. Working collaboratively via Booktype, an online editorial platform, has allowed both editors and contributors to explore new publishing technologies and gain an insight into the peer-review process.

The title and cover image of the book reflect our desire to emphasise the Nordic Research Network's role in bringing together individuals working in comparative isolation around the UK and further afield. As a small community of researchers, such a network is crucial for the dissemination of our work across academic and national borders. The Network has created a context in which light can be cast on the Nordic region both by these researchers themselves, and by the connections formed between them.

The papers, organised into thematic chapters, reflect and showcase the diversity of subject areas, approaches, and methodologies of the Nordic Studies postgraduate research community. Together, they help illuminate larger questions of how cultural, social, and historical identities are mediated through literature, historical narratives, films, and architecture.

Chapter One: Image and Artefact focuses on the construction and representation of identity through artefacts of the everyday. The papers in this chapter draw attention to the symbolic dimensions of narrative, architecture, and books. In 'The Many Guises of the Book – Genre and Paratext in the Works of Liza Marklund', Agnes Broomé dissects the performed paratextual identities of Liza Marklund's books in Sweden and the UK. Pei-Sze Chow and Essi Viitanen analyse cinematic representations of architectural spaces in 'Under the Scaffolding: Cinematic Representations of High-rise Buildings in Tapiola and Malmö' and argue for the relevance of film as an analytical tool in understanding spatial identities. Harriet Jean Evans shines a spotlight on the role and significance of the horse in 'The Horse and his Hero: A Symbiotic Relationship in Old Norse Literature', specifically examining its role as a symbol of a hero's heroic value.

Chapter Two: Methods and Sources focuses on the raw materials of textual analysis and their role in the construction of history. In his paper, 'Anthony Knipe: A Case Study of English Experience in Seventeenth Century Scandinavia', Adam Grimshaw discusses the unique experience of Englishman Anthony Knipe in two maritime centres in seventeenth century Scandinavia, as recorded in texts in Swedish and Norwegian archives. Björn Nordgren's paper 'Chancellor Oxenstierna's War 1635-1643: A Guide to Archival Sources' illustrates how under-researched archival sources can shed new light on the Thirty Years' War.

Chapter Three: Conflict and Society examines the idea of conflict within communities across space and time. In his paper 'Finnish National Identity and the Ingrian Right to Return Law: A Critical Discourse Analysis', Nicholas Prindiville investigates how Finnishness was constructed and defined within the Right to Return policy for Ingrian immigrants. Louisa Taylor's 'Granting Grið, Mercy and Peace: The Treatment of Opponents in War in Eleventh to Thirteenth Century Norway and Denmark' examines how elite men in these regions viewed restraint from killing defeated opponents as ideal, honourable conduct. In his paper 'Visibility, Authority, and Execution in *Heimskringla*', Keith Ruiter discusses what *Heimskringla* can tell us about how the judicial framework governing executions was perceived to have developed in medieval Scandinavia. Victoria Ralph's 'Landscapes of War and Vistas of Peace in "Margareta Fredkulla" by Selma Lagerlöf' is a study of how Lagerlöf uses the figure of Margareta Fredkulla to write back to a violent patriarchal version of Scandinavian history.

The final chapter, Author and Self-Image, focuses on individual authors and the negotiation of image and self-image via specific texts in their oeuvre. Ian Giles searches for a political Ingmar Bergman in the director's documentaries about Fårö, which reflect the complex interrelations between his personal, cinematic, and political interests. *Gengældelsens Veje*, Karen Blixen's only novel, is the subject of Barbara Tesio's paper, 'The Art of Entertaining a Nation under Nazi occupation: Pierre Andrézel and *Gengældelsens Veje*'. Her paper teases out the relationships between displacement, language, and the author's identity.

We hope you will enjoy reading the papers in this collection, and that the Nordic Research Network will continue to grow, nurture new generations of scholars, and inspire study of the Nordic region.

Finally, we would like to thank the following individuals for their invaluable help and guidance throughout the compilation of this book: Marita Fraser, Claire Thomson, and Elettra Carbone.

Biographies

Agnes Broomé is a PhD student at the Department of Scandinavian Studies at University College London. Her research examines the position of contemporary Swedish fiction on the British market from an interdisciplinary perspective. She holds an MA in Linguistics from the University of Edinburgh and an MA in Comparative Literature from University College London.

Pei-Sze Chow is a PhD student at University College London researching film and televisual representations of architecture and urban change in the Øresund region since the late 1990s. The project analyses how specific portrayals of the region's spatial development and discourses of a transnational identity emerge from shifts in socio-economic and cultural policies.

Harriet Jean Evans graduated from the University of York in January 2014. Her work focuses on medieval Scandinavia, and her Masters dissertation, supervised by Dr Matthew Townend, dealt with horse-hero relationships in Old Norse literature. She is currently researching the role of animals in the medieval Icelandic family.

Ian Giles is conducting PhD research on issues surrounding Scandinavian translation at the University of Edinburgh. He holds an MA (Hons) in Scandinavian Studies and an MSc in Translation Studies, both from the University of Edinburgh. He is a published literary and commercial translator of the Scandinavian languages.

Adam Grimshaw has received a full, three-year AHRC Doctoral Award in order to pursue his PhD thesis, entitled 'Anglo-Swedish Commercial Contact and Commodity Exchange in the Seventeenth Century'. His research also examines various other facets of British-Scandinavian associations in the seventeenth century.

Björn Nordgren is studying for a PhD at the University of St Andrews supervised by Professor Steve Murdoch. His project is entitled 'The Second Swedish Phase of the Thirty Years' War: 1635-43'. Björn is interested in seventeenth century Europe and questions of military revolution and change in particular.

Nicholas Prindiville is completing a PhD at the School of Slavonic and East European Studies, University College London, on the migration of Ingrians to Finland. Nicholas holds an MSc in European Studies from the London School of Economics and BA with honours in Political Science and German from Melbourne University.

Victoria Ralph graduated in 2007 from University College London with a BA in Humanities (Icelandic Studies). She is currently studying for an MPhil/PhD at University College London, researching the influence of Old Norse Literature on the Swedish author Selma Lagerlöf (1858-1940).

Keith Ruiter received his MA with distinction from the University of York's Centre for Medieval Studies. His research focuses on interdisciplinary approaches to considering outsiders, otherness, and social aspects of the Viking Age. He is currently seeking a place to pursue his PhD research.

Nichola Smalley is a PhD student at the Department of Scandinavian Studies, University College London. Her research focuses on the use of slang in rap and literature in Sweden and the UK, as well as the translation of literature that features such slang use.

Louisa Taylor holds a BA (Hons) and a Masters degree from the University of Birmingham and is currently studying for a PhD at University College London. Louisa's research compares the ideal behaviours adopted by elite men in the eleventh to thirteenth centuries as presented within historical narratives describing England, Norway and Denmark.

Barbara Tesio holds an MSc in Comparative Literature from the University of Edinburgh and is now pursuing a PhD at the same institution. Barbara's research concerns the works of Karen Blixen, with a particular focus on the relationship between language, displacement and identity.

Essi Viitanen is a PhD candidate at the Department of Scandinavian Studies at University College London. Her research examines representations of architecture and space in Finnish cinema. She holds an MA in Graphic Design from University of the Creative Arts, and BA in Media Arts from Royal Holloway, University of London.

The Many Guises of the Book – Genre and Paratext in the Works of Liza Marklund

Agnes Broomé
University College London

Introduction[1]

It may seem as though Scandinavian crime fiction, affectionately dubbed 'Scandi crime' or 'Nordic Noir' by both fans and protractors, has been inundating our book shops, newspapers, and television screens since time immemorial, but the broad popularity of this subgenre of crime fiction in fact only dates back to the late 1990s and the English-language publication of the first books in Henning Mankell's *Wallander* series. Moreover, it was not until almost a decade after that publication, as late as 2008-2009, that Stieg Larsson's *Millenium* trilogy helped Scandinavian crime fiction achieve the kind of iconic status it enjoys today, where its specific tropes and images have become well-known mainstream cultural memes. Consider, for example, the now famous, and oft-copied, woolly jumper worn by Sara Lund in the TV series *Forbrydelsen* (*The Killing*, 2007-2012).

I have argued elsewhere that the formation of genre in the case of Scandinavian crime fiction is driven not by textual similarity, which is what traditionally defines genre, but by paratextual identity.[2] In this paper I would like to take the opportunity to look at the ways in which publishers utilise the paratexts of books — i.e., the materials surrounding the main text of a work, such as cover design, endorsements, blurbs, and so forth — to establish and advertise generic identity.[3] To do this I will examine the authorship and publishing history of Swedish writer and journalist Liza Marklund. Aside from being a useful guide to branding and generic identity endowment, Marklund's oeuvre, both in the original Swedish and in English translation, is interesting because it demonstrates that a book's generic identity is, at least at the point of sale, decoupled from its actual text to a significant degree. Indeed, Marklund's *Annika Bengtzon* series and stand-alone crime novel *The Postcard Killers* show that genre, in the paratextual sense, far from being a fixed, textually inherent characteristic, behaves rather like an assigned, constructed value, a garment that can be donned or discarded according to the demands of the situation. It is a performed identity, which can be shaped and adjusted to suit the publishing context at hand, in order to attract a specific readership and, crucially, in order to maximise sales.

This paper will examine the ways in which literary works are endowed with generic identity and the ability to communicate said identity through their paratextual materials. It will also show that the generic identity signalled by a book's paratext can stand in relatively free relation to its text and that, consequently, generic identity must be considered fluid and adaptable. Finally, the paper will investigate the conditions under which a work's paratextual communication strategy may be seen to adapt and what type of alterations are likely to occur.

The *Annika Bengtzon* series

Still relatively unknown in the UK, in her native Sweden Liza Marklund has held a dominant position within crime writing since her crime debut in 1998. Her first crime novel, *Sprängaren* (*The Bomber*) was a runaway success, selling so many copies it became known as 'the Swedish bestseller of the century' (Berlin: 2006). *Sprängaren* also won several awards and established

Marklund as the undisputed queen of Swedish crime fiction. The *Annika Bengtzon* series, which at the time of writing consists of ten novels, including *Sprängaren*, have, together with Marklund's four stand-alone novels, sold over 15 million copies worldwide, been translated into thirty languages, and won a range of Swedish and international awards (Piratförlaget). In Sweden the books in the *Bengtzon* series, published by Piratförlaget, have a very distinctive look that makes them instantly recognisable both as the works of Marklund and as components of a cohesive series. Each book cover is dominated by a different colour and features a picture of the author herself as its most prominent graphic element. The titles of the books are very small compared to the name of the author, which is orthographically designed to emphasise the 'Z' in 'Liza', making it a central graphic element in itself. This highly recognisable style has become Marklund's calling card, her visual brand. In more recent Swedish paperback editions of the *Bengtzon* series, the covers have been revised, though we note that the designer, Eric Thunfors, has taken conspicuous care to preserve the strong branding elements of the original covers. The orthographic representation of Marklund's name has thus been retained, as have the relative prominence and size of it in relation to other graphic elements. The idea of working with one strong colour still forms a key part of the design, but the previously obligatory picture of the author on each cover has been dropped. The covers of Marklund's *Bengtzon* series cannot be said to draw heavily on any one generic trope, rather, they seem designed as a unique branding tool for the author and the series. The distinctive look signals that the first allegiance of the books' paratexts is to Marklund herself; she is the genre and brand they align with.[4]

The translation and publishing history of Marklund's oeuvre in the UK has not been as straightforward as its Swedish counterpart. Simon & Schuster acquired the rights and published Marklund's first four crime novels, *The Bomber* (*Sprängaren*), *Studio 69* (*Studio* sex), *Paradise* (*Paradiset*) and Prime Time between 2000 and 2006. The first three were published under the dedicated paperback imprint Pocket Books and the fourth under parent imprint Simon & Schuster. The series was then discontinued and languished until it was picked back up by Corgi, a Random House imprint, which bought the rights and commissioned new translations by Neil Smith. Beginning with *The Red Wolf* (*Röd varg*) in 2010, Corgi has published seven of the *Bengtzon* novels to date, with the next, *Borderline* (*Du gamla, du fria*), scheduled for publication in 2014.[5] Neither the Pocket Books nor the Corgi translations have sought to preserve the trademark look of the Swedish editions. Given that the paratextual strategy of the Swedish series was essentially self-referential, and acknowledging that Liza Marklund does not function as a recognisable brand in the UK, due to the lack of name-recognition, the decision to adjust the paratextual strategy for the UK context is hardly surprising. In order to appeal to consumers in the UK, Marklund's books needed to be endowed with a recognisable identity that could resonate with book buyers and critics.

Pocket Books' Marklund covers cannot be said to form any coherent entity. The first two are dark, using architectural imagery to create a sense of confinement and suspense. The third and fourth are almost entirely white. The third, *Paradise*, retains an architectural element at its core, but the scene, a street in what looks like the old centre of an attractive European city, evokes through the use of perspective a sense of endlessness and space that stands in stark contrast to the atmosphere of the first two covers. By the fourth book, *Prime Time*, the cover design conforms entirely to what had by this time – 2006 – become a fixed Scandinavian crime fiction trope: a slightly blue-tinted, white, snowy landscape, flat and empty as far as the eye can see but for the dark silhouette of a lone person in the distance, the title announced in big, bold, red letters.[6] The only element retained from any of the previous books is the font and size of Marklund's name, which is consistent with the cover of *Paradise*.[7]

In terms of paratextual design, Corgi picked up right where Pocket Books left off, firmly aligning Marklund's books with the Scandinavian crime genre, which had only been gaining in popularity since Pocket Books' final Marklund venture in 2006. The first title published by Corgi was *The Red Wolf*. The striking red cover of the Swedish book, with its evocations of Maoist China (pivotal to the plot) and prominent photograph of Marklund front and centre, gave way to a cover which by this time must be considered blandly clichéd: the blue-tinted, bleak, deserted landscape, falling snow blurring the focus, and bold red lettering. *Exposed (Studio sex)*, the second title to be published by Corgi, was given a more threatening, but only very slightly more imaginative cover: here the colour scheme centres on the rich orange of sunset, but the overall design concept, built around an empty but threatening, wintry rural landscape, remains unaltered. The third title, *The Bomber*, reverts entirely to type with a cover that is barely distinguishable from that of *The Red Wolf*.

By the fourth title, *Vanished* (*Paradiset*), however, Corgi decided to take the series' paratext in a new direction. They did away with the frosty, flat, deserted Swedish landscape and replaced it with the backlit outline of a woman. In terms of cover design, *Vanished* occupies an interesting transitional space within the Corgi series. Though the motif is a radical departure from the empty landscapes of the first three books, Corgi has clearly been keen to make the transition smooth for book buyers conditioned to identify conventional Scandinavian crime covers. Thus, the feeling of openness and endlessness are retained, as is the characteristic snowy foreground and the white blurriness it inevitably entails. Likewise, the orthographic elements conform to Scandinavian crime convention and the previous three books with its big, bold, crimson letters. The transition initiated with the cover of *Vanished* is then completed with the cover of book five, *Last Will* (*Nobels testamente*), which in compositional terms is almost identical to its immediate predecessor but bears little resemblance to the first three books. Like *Vanished*, it features a fairly nondescript background and a backlit woman front and centre. Where *Vanished* was bright white and deliberately blurred, however, *Last Will* plays with sharp, straight lines and the stark contrast between harsh white light and pressing darkness. The one feature retained from the previous Bengtzon books is the prominent red orthography.

This fairly drastic design change has a profound effect on the identity of the *Bengtzon* series and signals a conscious attempt to shift the series and Marklund from run-of-the-mill Scandinavian crime to something altogether more literary. In order to achieve that effect, the publisher draws on familiar paratextual tropes belonging to the realm of literary fiction, rather than on tropes of Scandinavian crime. The trope in question is a woman's back. Traditionally reserved for pulp fiction and chick-lit, this motif has become so ubiquitous on the covers of literary titles of all persuasions in the last few years that it has even occasioned a trend study in *The New York Times* (Schama, 2013).[8] Using such a motif on the cover of *Last Will* means that the book describes and advertises itself to consumers as literary fiction first and Scandinavian crime second; it has visually adopted a new generic identity.

Marklund's *Bengtzon* series thus demonstrates how visual aspects of the paratext can be used by a publisher to strongly and obviously signal the generic identity of a book and an authorship. In the Swedish context the most important genre, or brand, to refer to is Marklund herself. The cover design of the Swedish editions of her books are unapologetically self-referential, establishing Marklund's oeuvre as a strong, recognisable brand that consumers are familiar with and can base purchasing decisions on. In the UK context, the paratexts of the Pocket Books editions show that the British publisher did not believe the Marklund-focused marketing pitch would work on the British market, presumably because of her lack of name-recognition in that country. Instead, the first three books seem geared toward a general, rather under-defined, and therefore flexible, non-prescriptive crime style. By the end of Pocket Books' Marklund venture, however, Scandinavian crime had begun to crystallise as a sub-genre of crime fiction, giving publishers access to a suddenly widely recognisable visual language that communicates the identity of the new sub-genre. This broad literary and market development finds concrete expression in the cover design of Pocket Books' final Marklund title, *Prime Time*.

Corgi, in turn, took full advantage of the new visual language of Scandinavian crime when publishing the first three *Bengtzon* books, tapping into the Scandinavian crime fiction fever which had, by 2010, completely swept the UK. The two books that followed, however, reveal a change of strategy. No longer satisfied to brand Marklund simply as a Scandinavian crime author, Corgi chose to adjust the generic signals broadcast by the paratexts of *Vanished* and *Last Will*, drawing more heavily on literary paratextual cues. Speculation about the reasons for this change unfortunately lie outside the scope of this article, but whatever the rationale, the change of course reveals that generic identity, so far as it is signalled by paratextual elements, is fluid, not fixed, the result of detachable extra-textual factors rather than inherent textual characteristics. The visual paratext cannot only be used to define a text, but to redefine it and cast it in a different generic light. Thus, a textually coherent series of novels, such as Marklund's *Bengtzon* series, can pledge allegiance to a number of genres by changing its visual generic markers, allowing it to seek out a range of audiences.

The Postcard Killers

An even more remarkable example of paratextual adaptation can be found in the covers of one of Marklund's stand-alone crime novels, *Postcard Killers* (*The Postcard Killers*, 2010).[9] *The Postcard Killers* is unique among Marklund's works because it was co-authored with American crime/thriller titan James Patterson. The paratexts of the different editions of the book are of particular interest to this discussion because they illustrate very clearly the ways in which paratextual cues can be adapted to signal a generic identity deemed desirable by the publisher, rather than one predetermined by the nature of the text. Moreover, they reveal the extent to which publishers seek to align their titles with established, familiar tropes that facilitate clear and direct identity communication with consumers.

The Swedish editions of *Postcard Killers* (the hardback and paperback editions are practically identical) are strikingly dark; the larger part of each is black. Only in the middle of the covers is there some light; an isolated old-fashioned lantern seems to defy the darkness that has engulfed the rest of the cover, illuminating a small patch of the ochre stone wall on which it is mounted. The title of the book is remarkably minute and the colour of the letters is fairly similar to that of the background graphics, making it unobtrusive to the point of being obscure, while the names of Marklund and Patterson — Marklund at the top and Patterson at the bottom — loom large. It is a sedate cover that seems not to want to signal much other than a fairly highbrow crime identity, the cousin of P.D. James' or Elizabeth George's works, perhaps. It is interesting to note that the cover design makes no reference at all to Marklund's distinctive Swedish oeuvre even though it deliberately attempts to harness her fame and brand recognition by billing her over Patterson, who is, despite his international success, less well-known in Sweden.

The English-language hardback edition of *The Postcard Killers* is also dark, though the general impression is livelier than the Swedish cover. The lit part of the cover is no longer centrally placed, but occupies instead the top quarter of the cover. The image retains the colour scheme of the Swedish editions, but rather than a stationary lantern on a wall, the illustration is of two people running, backlit, up a narrow cobbled alley, away from the camera, toward light and infinity. Similarly to the Swedish editions, the main feature of the English-language front cover is the text. Here, though, the most prominent text is that of the title, which is centrally placed, very large and bright red. James Patterson's name is displayed above the title and Liza Marklund's below. A cursory investigation of Patterson's other titles, especially the ones which were co-authored with other writers, reveals that the design concept, and the orthography in particular, corresponds closely to other Patterson titles, such as *NYPD Red* (2013), *Confessions of a Murder Suspect* (2013), *Kill Me if You Can* (2013), *Honeymoon* (2011), *Private London* (2012), *Private Games* (2012), *4th of July* (2009), and *Judge and Jury* (2011). In brief, though some small concessions to the Swedish edition have been made, *The Postcard Killers* essenially looks like a James Patterson novel.[10]

The impression that Liza Marklund is relatively incidental to the marketing of *The Postcard Killers*, that the book is treated, paratextually, as simply part of Patterson's production, is reinforced by an examination of the English-language paperback edition. Here, any reference to Sweden, where *Postcard Killers* is in fact set and which has provided Marklund's other English-language books with their most obvious paratextual identity, has been completely erased. While the photograph on the cover of the hardback edition looks as though it may have been taken in Stockholm, the image on the paperback edition features as its most prominent element the Eiffel Tower and the Champ de Mars. A blonde woman occupies the foreground and most of the cover is overlaid with orthography; the title is the most dominant feature and Patterson's name is once again listed at the top, adjacent to the title, and Marklund's at the bottom, below the image. The font is identical to the one used on the hardback edition, which is to say identical to the one used on many of Patterson's other books. At first, we might be fooled into assuming that the blonde woman recalls Marklund's habit of appearing on her Swedish book covers, but we soon realise that this is coincidental; the blonde woman in the foreground is in fact a Patterson trope. Indeed, the paperback edition of *The Postcard Killers* is very nearly identical to other paperback Patterson covers published under the Arrow imprint of Random House, particularly *Now You See Her* (2012). So similar, indeed, is that to *The Postcard Killers* that it is difficult to tell them apart at all.

It is clear that the English-language editions of *The Postcard Killers* take practically no notice of Marklund's authorship or unique branding and that the visual language habitually used to signal Scandinavian crime is entirely absent as well. While 'Liza Marklund' is the identity appealed to by the Swedish editions of the *Bengtzon* series, and 'Scandinavian crime' the identity most obviously tapped into by their English-language counterparts, *The Postcard Killers* cleaves to the 'James Patterson' identity. What this demonstrates is that publishers are able to choose from a range of genres, tropes, and branding cues when designing the graphic elements of a paratext. The appearance of a particular paratext is not directly or inflexibly dictated by its text. Because book covers are the most immediate and direct channel of communication with consumers, who have presumably learnt to judge books by their covers, they are used to align individual titles, series, or whole authorships with the genre, trope, or brand the publisher deems most likely to maximise sales. Thus, Marklund's fame and name-recognition is exploited in Sweden but the popularity and visual distinctiveness of Scandinavian crime is appealed to in the

UK, unless, of course, an even stronger brand is available. With US book sales that exceed the combined efforts of John Grisham, Stephen King, and Dan Brown, and with 14 million copies sold annually worldwide, James Patterson is just such a brand.[11]

Conclusion

Fiction books are curious products; unlike many other consumer goods, each product, or title, is an entity unique unto itself. This inevitably makes the branding and marketing of fiction difficult; it is, in other words, diffcult for publishers to inform potential buyers about the content of the product in an accessible way. To exacerbate matters, consumers nowadays face practically infinite choice whenever they enter a bookshop, making the need for accurate and succinct product information all the more imperative. One of the tools publishers use to communicate with and inform potential buyers about the nature of a book is the book's cover design. It is not enough for a cover to be beautiful or inviting; in order to maximise a title's market success, it needs to signal what kind of product it adorns. Book covers fill this function by establishing the book's identity referentially, through the use of visual cues that situate the work within familiar, recognisable frames of reference. Thus, a book can, by means of paratextual markers, signal its alignment with, to take but a few examples, the romance genre, its suitability for male readers, its appropriateness for a certain age group, and so on. Covers can be seen to function, then, as a kind of visual shorthand, helping potential buyers and readers to understand what kind of text they are looking at. In this sense they participate in a branding process that aims to inform consumers that 'you can confidently purchase this book because the cover tells you that it is similar to other books with which you are already familiar'.

Crucially, however, the visual elements of paratexts are not strictly dictated by the text. A text can be, and more often than not is, given different paratextual appearances in different editions. This means that the paratextual identity of a text is open to interpretation and recalibration. A text can be crime fiction in one edition and women's literature in the next; it can shift from pulp to high-brow and back again; from young adult to literary fiction to fantasy, with all that this entails in terms of readership, critical response, bookshop placement, eligibility for awards consideration, and so forth. In this article I wanted to show what such a journey might look like; the works of Liza Marklund reveal not only the ways in which publishers strive to establish firm and informative identities for their titles and series, but also the ways in which publishers are able, and willing, to manipulate those identities for reasons of their own.

Notes

[1] This paper draws on the research into the publishing and marketing contexts of contemporary Swedish fiction that underpins my doctoral thesis.

[2] For a discussion of the generic status of Scandinavian crime fiction, see Broomé (forthcoming).

[3] For reasons of space constraints, the only paratextual feature analysed and discussed in this article will be cover design; for a more detailed discussion of aspects of the paratext cf. Genette (1997).

[4] It should be noted that Liza Marklund is a co-founder and co-owner of the publishing house, Piratförlaget, that publishes her novels in Sweden. Undoubtedly this has had an impact on the author's opportunity to be involved in decisions pertaining to paratextual design.

[5] It has not been possible for me to take Marklund's two most recent

novels, *Lifetime* and *The Long Shadow*, both published this year, into account in this study.

[6] The list of Nordic authors whose covers (particularly the editions published around this period) conform to this pattern could be made very long indeed, a few examples include: Håkan Nesser, Arnaldur Indriðasson, Jo Nesbø, Henning Mankell, Karin Fossum, Åsa Larsson, Camilla Läckberg, Åke Edwardsson, Mari Jungstedt, Yrsa Sigurðadóttir, Anne Holt, and Kjell Eriksson.

[7] Interestingly, Simon & Schuster released a new edition of *Prime Time* in 2011, with a new cover. For this edition, the snowy, deserted Scandinavian crime trope of the first edition, which was so popular in 2006, has been abandoned in favour of the Scandinavian crime trope that was the height of fashion in 2011, the 'Stieg Larsson' trope. This paratextual template dictates that a book be either red, green or blue, that it feature a close-up of a dark-haired woman's face, that the author's name and the title be very prominent and that the letters of one of these be white and the other in colour. Interesting comparisons can be made to Pan's rebranding Håkan Nesser's van Veeteren series and the 2009-2011 Vintage editions of Jo Nesbø's *Harry Hole* series.

[8] As was the case with the 'Frigid North' trope discussed in note 5 above, the list of authors whose recent book covers utilise the 'Woman's Back' trope is nigh endless. A few examples: *Finding Casey*, by Jo-Ann Mapson; *The Unruly Passion of Eugénie R.*, by Carole DeSanti; *The Headmaster's Wager*, by Vincent Lam; *The Pretty One*, by Lucinda Rosenfeld; *The Smart One*, by Jennifer Close; *Beautiful Day*, by Elin Hilderbrand; *In One Person*, by John Irving; *While the Women Are Sleeping*, by Javier Marías; *Living, Thinking, Looking*, by Siri Hustvedt, *The Crimson Petal and the White*, by Michael Farber; *Anatomy of a Disapperance*, by Hisham Matar.

[9] The book is inconsistently entitled either *The Postcard Killers* or just *Postcard Killers* in its various English-language editions. In this paper I will, for the sake of clarity and consistency, term the Swedish-language edition *Postcard Killers* and its English-language counterpart *The Postcard Killers*.

[10] It should be noted, of course, that the English-language edition of *The Postcard Killers* was first published by Little, Brown and Company, which also publishes the rest of Patterson's literary output, a fact likely to have had some impact on design choices.

[11] See Mahler, Jonathan. 'James Patterson Inc.' January 20, 2010, *The New York Times*. http://www.nytimes.com/2010/01/24/magazine/24patterson-t.html?pagewanted=all&_r=0.

Works Cited

Berlin, Jessica. 'Liza Marklunds Sprängaren, en studie över genusperspektivet i Sprängaren'. Högskolan Kristianstad, lärarutbildningen, 2006.

Broome, Agnes. 'Judging a Book by its Cover: Is Scandinavian crime fiction a genre?', in *True North*, Ed. B. J. Epstein, forthcoming.

Genette, Gerard. *Paratexts: Thresholds of Interpretation*. Cambridge: Cambridge University Press, 1997.

Larsson, Stieg. *The Girl with the Dragon Tattoo*. London: Quercus, 2008.

---. *The Girl Who Played with Fire*. London: Quercus, 2009.

---. *The Girl Who Kicked the Hornets' Nest*. London: Quercus, 2009.

Marklund, Liza. *Sprängaren*. Stockholm: Piratförlaget, 1998.

---. *Studio sex*. Stockholm: Piratförlaget, 1999.

---. *Paradiset*. Stockholm: Piratförlaget, 2000.

---. *Prime Time*. Stockholm: Piratförlaget, 2002.

---. *Den Röda Vargen*. Stockholm: Piratförlaget, 2003.

---. *Nobels testamente*. Stockholm: Piratförlaget, 2006.

---. *Livstid*. Stockholm: Piratförlaget, 2007.

---. *The Bomber*, trans. Kajsa von Hofsten. Pocket Books, 2000.

---. *Studio 69*, trans. Kajsa von Hofsten. Pocket Books, 2002.

---. *Paradise*, trans. Ingrid Eng-Rundlow. Pocket Books, 2004.

---. *Prime Time*, trans. Ingrid Eng-Rundlow. Simon & Schuster, 2006.

---. *The Red Wolf*, trans. Neil Smith. Corgi, 2010.

---. *The Bomber*, trans. Neil Smith. Corgi 2011.

---. *Exposed*, trans. Neil Smith. Corgi, 2011.

---. *Vanished*, trans. Neil Smith. Corgi, 2012.

---. *Last Will*, trans. Neil Smith. Corgi, 2012.

---. *Lifetime*, trans. Neil Smith. Corgi, 2013.

Marklund, Liza and James Patterson. *Postcard Killers*. Stockholm: Piratförlaget, 2010.

Patterson, James and Liza Marklund. *The Postcard Killers*. New York: Little, Brown and Company, 2010.

Piratförlaget. 'Fakta om Liza Marklund'. 17 January 2014. <http://www.piratforlaget.se/liza-marklund/fakta-om-liza-marklund/>

Schama, Chloe. 'Show Some Spine' in *The New York Times*. 20 June 2013. 17 January 2014. <http://www.nytimes.com/2013/06/23/books/review/show-some-spine.html?nl=books&emc=edit_bk_20130621&_r=1&>

Mahler, Jonathan. 'James Patterson Inc.' in *The New York Times*. 20 January 2010. 17 January 2014. <http://www.nytimes.com/2010/01/24/magazine/24patterson-t.html?pagewanted=all&_r=0>

Under the Scaffolding: Cinematic Representations of High-rise Buildings in Tapiola and Malmö

Pei-Sze Chow and Essi Viitanen
University College London

The subject of this paper was first presented as a dialogue between Pei-Sze Chow and Essi Viitanen at the Nordic Research Network conference.

Introduction

This paper grew from an ongoing exchange of ideas between two research projects that seek to understand the multifaceted representations of architecture as depicted on film and in television. In this essay, we analyse two examples of Nordic landmarks and the ways in which these are interpreted and re-imagined on screen. In both examples, Tapiola in Finland and Malmö in Sweden, the focus is on innovative welfare state residential housing projects that have been pioneering in their vision for redefining Nordic social housing.

Both examples draw on Michel de Certeau's 1997 work *Walking in the City*, in which he differentiates the experience of looking at the city and that of walking through it:

> An Icarus flying above these waters, he can ignore the devices of Daedalus in mobile and labyrinths far below. His elevation transfigures him into a voyeur.

[...]

> The ordinary practitioners of the city live 'down below,' below the thresholds at which visibility begins. They walk – an elementary form of this experience of the city; they are walkers, Wandersmänner, whose bodies follow the thicks and thins of an urban 'text' they write without being to read it. (1997: 92-93)

Describing looking down at the Manhattan city grid from the 110th floor of the World Trade Centre, de Certeau argues that this elevated viewpoint allows him to read the city visually, similar to the same scopic drive that 'haunts users of architectural productions by materialising today the utopia that yesterday was only painted' (ibid. 92). He sees the city through the perspective of the 'totalizing eye' of architects and planners – as a perfected 'panorama city' to be gazed upon. However, de Certeau writes that it is necessary to 'disentangle' ourselves from this 'voyeur-god' perspective, and he argues for an experience of the city from 'down below'. In other words, seeing becomes an impediment to understanding and experiencing 'hidden and familiar meanings' in the various pockets of lived spaces that are only made apparent through walking (ibid. 104). These forms of operation transform the space by misappropriation through misappreciation as walkers reinterpret the cityscape, weaving their own paths among the buildings.

We draw on film as an analytical tool to make visible this disconnect between planned space and lived space, as described by de Certeau. Through our discussion of the two residential sites, their planned attributes, and the representations of these buildings on film, we show how the cinematic reworkings of these sites present an alternative dimension of social commentary and criticism that are otherwise absent from the planned vision of the spaces.

Tapiola

> Täyttäköön tähän nouseva puutarhakaupunki siihen kiinnitetyt toiveet ja olkoon se voimakkaana sysäyksenä asuntopoliittiselle kehitykselle koko maassa. (Von Hertzen, 1984: 53)
>
> (Let the garden city which rises here fulfill the hopes we have for it, and let it be a strong launch for the development of housing policy in the whole nation.)[1]

These hopeful words form the final sentence of the charter of Tapiola, laid into the ground alongside the foundation stone in the official groundbreaking ceremony of Tapiola on 5 September 1953. They launched the building of Finland's first garden city, which defined the white modernist aesthetic of Finnish suburban high-rise developments (ibid. 219). Located on the outskirts of Helsinki, this was an area where plans carefully devised by famed Finnish architects came to life; where Otto-Iivari Meurman's (1954) theories on suburban settlements served as a basis for townplanning, and Aarne Ervi's award-winning design for the Keskusallas, a central water feature complete with fountains, was realised. Tapiola was also the culmination of Heikki von Hertzen's vision for progressive suburban housing, which provided inhabitants with a healthy living environment away from the dust and noise of central Helsinki. Von Hertzen, the executive director of the housing organisation Asuntosäätiö, which was in charge of developing Tapiola, had already outlined his views on the future of housing in his 1947 book *Koti vaiko kasarmi lapsillemme* (*Homes or Barracks for our Children*). This new area was to become a model of architectural elegance, whilst setting the benchmark for egalitarian housing policy (von Herzen, 1984). In many ways Tapiola succeeded in this, as Asko Salokorpi described it as 'a model for success' in the field of social planning (1970:

45). This suburb of white high-rises on the outskirts of Helsinki became known as a showcase of Finnish architectural skill and an attraction to show foreign visitors (von Herzen, 1984).

In the 1960s, a decade after building started, the suburban town of Tapiola sparked an interest among filmmakers, such as Maunu Kurkvaara and Jaakko Pakkasvirta. Their films captured the architectural glory of the newly built area whilst simultaneously developing the cinematic style of Finnish New Wave filmmaking. This new style of cinema broke away from the conventions of the rural melodramas of the studio system and focused on examining the urban experience (Toiviainen, 1975). Kurkvaara and Pakkasvirta's films marvel at modernist architecture and high-rise housing, whilst exposing the viewer to a darker and more sinister side of the suburban experience. Films such as Kurkvaara's *Yksityisalue* (*Private Property*, 1962) and Pakkasvirta's *Vihreä Leski* (*The Green Widow*, 1968) render the landmarks and skyline of Tapiola into their cinematic landscape and set a localised stage for fictive storylines.

Kurkvaara's *Yksityisalue* begins with the suicide of its protagonist, the architect Koski, and follows his young colleague's investigation into the events that lead to Koski's death. Whilst recounting Koski's last days, the film touches upon the planning process of the suburbs and the moral dilemmas of mass housing. Architecture is ever present in the film. Drawings of buildings decorate the walls of the architect's office, we browse through books on Le Corbusier, visit an exhibition showcasing Oscar Niemeyer's work, and watch Koski's hand as he sketches towering high-rises. The viewer is privy to arguments with developers over cutting corners on the design in order to reach profit margins. Koski's voiceover recounts designing suburban housing, his despair over the ready-made slums they are building, and his disillusionment with his own profession. Despite the film using architecture as a prominent theme throughout, it remains viewed only from the perspective of the designer. *Yksityisalue* does not show a single inhabitant occupying the new buildings, but instead draws attention to the problematic role of the architect and the financial constraints of the construction process.

Whilst most of *Yksityisalue*'s architecture exists on paper, in books or at a construction sites covered in scaffolding, the shot of Tapiola introduces the finished product in all its measured and pristine glory. Kurkvaara introduces the viewer to Tapiola through its architectural landmarks. The protagonist Koski and his muse drive to Tapiola and pull up by Aarne Ervi's instantly recognizable the water feature. The camera moves in vertical pans drawing attention to the upward lines of the crisp white high-rise buildings. The couple's arrival is followed directly by a shot of them from high above the street level enjoying the views from one of the central high-rises. They sit by a window, which frames a perfectly symmetrical landscape of woodland, bold high-rises, and perfectly straight roads. As de Certeau describes looking down at the uniform beauty of the Manhattan city grid, experiencing the harmonious and precise geometry of roads and buildings (1997: 91), *Kurkvaara* shifts the perspective in a similar manner. A skyline of memorable landmarks is transformed by a shift in vantage point. The scene gives one of the film's few glimpses of modernist architecture in its finished form.

Pakkasvirta's *Vihreä Leski* also uses Tapiola as its setting, but this time showing the experiences of a housewife living in the area. The opening of the film shows a documentary-style interview with a local inhabitant. The woman praises the area as a nice place to live in, whilst the camera guides the viewer through Tapiola's architectural landmarks. Similar to *Kurkvaara*, *Pakkasvirta* introduces the milieu through the familiar landmarks of Tapiola centre, but his camera remains on the street level, following the pedestrians past buildings and into the domestic sphere.

In *Vihreä Leski* the modernist architecture serves as a backdrop to isolation, depression, and an overarching theme of voyeurism and surveillance. Landmarks become a façade which hide a more fragmented and troubled experience of Tapiola. The forest, which von Hertzen hoped would bring residents closer to nature (1984), is now the domain of a peeping tom who is a constant unsettling presence. The welfare state show home is transformed into a dark and oppressive place. The camera in *Vihreä Leski* moves on ground level following the characters as they wander through the space, or assumes the point of view of a peeping tom in the forest. It shows the isolation of those who live in Tapiola, a selection of lonely figures, sectioned off in a grid of identical windows.

Moving from *Yksityisalue*'s harmonious spatial geometry, viewed from on high, to the paranoia of walking through dark woods in *Vihreä Leski*, the cinematic reimaginings of Tapiola echo de Certeau's 'Icarian fall' (1997: 92). Both films capture the initial optimism and private fears of adjusting to an unfamiliar suburban lifestyle, whilst drawing attention to the wide gulf between the planned environment and the experience of living in it. *Kurkvaara* highlights the aesthetic beauty of the 'panorama-city' of Tapiola, and comments on the problematic nature of realising the planned vision for suburban housing. *Pakkasvirta* introduces the planned space, but delves into the 'down-below', showing the intimate everyday interactions between the walker and her surroundings. The portrayals of both films problematise the suburban milieu and draw attention to the disconnect between the place and its residents.

Turning Torso

'Välkommen till Malmös landmärke.'

'Welcome to Malmö's landmark.' The phrase greets the visitor upon loading the HSB Turning Torso's official website. Elsewhere on Sweden and Malmö's tourism websites, the Turning Torso appears either in an unassuming pose at the centre of a tranquil waterfront development, or shot from a worm's-eye angle drenched in all colours of the rainbow promoting the top eleven gay-friendly places to visit in Malmö. From virtual spaces to the physical space itself, the Turning Torso is ever-present and dominates the visual field: while walking around Malmö, you are always playing hide-and-seek with the skyscraper, and whether you are flying into Kastrup, hiking in Lund, or watching a television crime drama series set in Öresund, a view of the building is unavoidable. While also serving as a navigational tool and a symbol of the city's rejuvenated character, the Turning Torso's twisted shape is typically depicted in the media as a cool, cosmopolitan artefact in urban Malmö. What is unseen, however, are the internal conflicts and tensions that constitute the place. *Sossen, arkitekten och det skruvade huset* (*The Socialist, The Architect and the Twisted Tower*), the 2005 documentary by Fredrik Gertten tracing the building's genesis, makes visible the disconnect between the planned vision for the building and its reception by the local community.

The Turning Torso was first conceived by world-renowned 'starchitect' Santiago Calatrava as a sculpture that accompanied his entry for the architectural competition for the Öresund Bridge project in 1999. The idea to translate the design into a residential skyscraper in Malmö's new Western Harbour district was proposed by Jonny Örbäck, then-Managing Director of Hyresgästernas sparkasse och byggnadsförening (HSB), one of Sweden's largest housing organisations and co-operatives. Construction began in 2001 and was finally completed four years later, with many lauding its architectural innovations.

As is expected of large-scale prestige projects, the construction process for the Turning Torso was not without its controversies. This included negative reactions to its architectural design, engineering challenges, an ever-increasing budget, the delayed schedule, and declining interest from buyers of the apartments over time. While these concerns are certainly no different from other projects of starchitectural status,[2] what made the Turning Torso a contentious topic was the state's branding of the project as the city's new landmark. It was to replace Malmö's beloved landmark, the Kockums crane, which was due to be dismantled (*Guide: Western Harbour. Sustainable City Development*, 2009: 4). Inhabitants of Malmö had come to form strong emotional attachments to the crane, which was also the subject of one of Gertten's documentaries set in the region, *Bye Bye Malmö* (2002).[3] In its place, the Turning Torso was to be several things at once: a landmark for inhabitants of the city, an architectural shorthand for Malmö (and to a certain extent, the Öresund region), and a new beacon of the city's post-industrial modernisation and transformation from a working-class community into a white-collar knowledge-based economy. In Malmö's tourism material, images of the Turning Torso dominate websites and brochures, while also featuring regularly in film and television productions, *Bron/Broen* (*The Bridge*, 2011–2013) and the 2013 Eurovision Song Contest broadcast being recent examples. Embedded within the city council's emphasis on sustainable development, these representations of the Turning Torso contribute to a coherent image and narrative of Malmö as a 'City of Tomorrow', attracting various streams of human and cultural capital and commercial investment (Jansson, 2005: 1672; Tryggestad and Georg, 2001: 188).

The Turning Torso
Source: wikipedia.org/wiki/
Photographer:Väsk

To say the design of the Turning Torso is unique is an understatement. In the context of Swedish housing design, the construction of the residential skyscraper certainly broke away from tradition and presented a radical and perhaps even provocative interpretation of Swedish residential housing. As noted by architecture commentator Paul Goldberger in *The New Yorker*, the building's design is out of sync with the rest of the immediate surroundings and there is 'little interest in connecting to street life' (2005). Its distinctive design by an international architect was certainly no guarantee for a warm welcome by the locals, as is made very clear in the dramatic narrative of *Sossen, arkitekten och det skruvade huset*, particularly in scenes where HSB shareholders expressed their firm dislike of the building alongside a lack of faith in Örbäck as a leader. The documentary charts the various struggles faced by Örbäck to deliver the building on time and within budget, and to convince the HSB stakeholders of the Turning Torso's relevance to Malmö while managing the tensions between the Swedish engineering and construction team and Calatrava and his team of architects. By the end of the film, Örbäck is forced to resign while the completed building goes on to win international awards.

The film comes to an end just as the building begins to come to life, as it were. The only full images of Turning Torso within the film are the various planned and symbolic representations of the building, particularly in the form of architectural sketches and models, the original sculpture, and Calatrava's commentary on the building's design being inspired by the movement of the human body. Calatrava's voice commands this narrative of the building as a desirable 'body' and inspiration for its inhabitants and the local community, and throughout the film, we see the design process of this body as it is being constructed. Örbäck emphasises in the film also that the Turning Torso is an opportunity to revitalise standards of housing in Sweden: 'We see this as housing's

Formula One today. We want it to be the standard tomorrow.' Indeed, these are idealised images from the perspectives of the architect, the planners, builders, and developers. To underscore this conceptualisation of the building, the film features grand long-shots of the Turning Torso from a distance, from a ground-level perspective looking upwards, or panning across the wider landscape with the building prominently standing out amidst the flatter silhouette of the Western Harbour. While these images create a sense of awe and monumentality, they also project a sense of the building as uninhabited and notably void of human activity. Furthermore, the camera is not allowed inside the completed building, the architect and builders have moved on to other projects, and all the film is able to capture is an emphatic rendering of the Turning Torso as a landmark from afar, and nothing else. Writing about the Öresund rhetoric, Orvar Löfgren suggests that popular visions of the region using enthusiastic language of cosmopolitanism and progressiveness 'run the risk of turning into empty rhetoric, a trivial cliché, as in the hyped poetics of event management or place marketing' (2000: 53). In a similar vein, the film seems to project an ambivalence regarding the building's relationship with its locality.

The film, produced and funded by various local (Film i Skåne, Malmö Kulturstöd) and foreign organisations,[4] might therefore be interpreted as a reflection on the various identity constructions for this new urban space that was only just in the process of coming into being in the early 2000s. Throughout the course of the film, we see the Turning Torso co-opted by various actors – first by Örbäck and then Calatrava, and after Örbäck's resignation, the larger HSB Malmö community comes around to the idea of it being a symbol of rejuvenation for the city. On the one hand, it is a local prestige project driven by economic imperatives to direct attention to a rejuvenated Malmö, southern Sweden, and the transnational Öresund region. Indeed, the building has also been adopted by various state actors for the place-marketing of the Öresund region, alongside the Öresund Bridge (Eskilsson and Högdahl, 2009: 76). On the other hand, the international success of its architecture has also confirmed the city's position as 'a node in the global network society' (Jansson, 2005: 1672).

Conclusions

In the first instance, the films discussed in this essay are physical fragments of the respective moments in the histories of the sites. As moving image artefacts that capture the processes of urban change, these films are also in dialogue with the rhetoric surrounding the buildings. Apart from contributing to the public discourse that surrounds the buildings, the films also present an opportunity for viewers to critically reflect on questions of place identity and the motivations and meanings projected onto such landmark architectural projects. An example of this role of architecture as social catalyst is the fervent debate on suburban lifestyle and architecture that Vihreä Leski sparked in the press (Miettinen, 1968; Talvi, 1968; Tuomikoski, 1968; Eteläpää, 1968; Luoma, 1968). Pietari Kääpä (2013) argues that early Finnish cinema used Helsinki's architectural wonders 'as a way to support Finnish self-conceptions of cosmopolitanism' and notes how the films of the 1960s and 1970s captured the social problems and changes in lifestyle caused by migration to Helsinki from rural areas. The dual nature of Tapiola as both an architectural wonder of modernism and a symbol for urbanisation and mass migration is captured in the ways in which Kurkvaara and Pakkasvirta transport the architecture onto the screen. *Sossen, arkitekten och det skruvade huset* is only one of Gertten's several documentary projects examining various aspects of Malmö life - the local football team, the dismantling of the Kockums crane, and the construction of the Öresund bridge. This particular collection of films forms a visual tapestry of the life and space of the region, and offers alternative visions and critical interpretations of the official narratives surrounding various public spaces and entities. Indeed, while some of the debates documented in Sossen, arkitekten och det skruvade huset were certainly reported in the news media, the film presents an otherwise unseen view of the personal, cultural, and ideological conflicts that are woven into the construction of the building.

Secondly, whether fiction or documentary, films go beyond simply documenting the buildings in which they are set. Cinema's capacity to communicate sound, movement, and even touch, allows it to bridge the gap between the acts of viewing architecture and experiencing it. The interaction between the characters and their surroundings can make visible the spatial practices of everyday life. Similarly, the camera itself can take an active role within the space, wandering through and gazing at the architecture. This cinematic landscape is an intricate and rich one that can facilitate a dialogue between real and imagined spaces. As de Certeau writes, 'the panorama-city is a "theoretical" (that is, visual) simulacrum, in short a picture, whose condition of possibility is an oblivion and a misunderstanding of practices' (1997: 93). In describing the disconnect between the planned cityscape, viewed from afar, and the experience of travelling through it on foot, he suggests that the city is transformed from a visual experience to an embodied one as the perspective shifts from a viewer to a flâneur (ibid. 92). Cinema is unique in its capacity to articulate these misunderstood practices of urban architecture in a visual medium, expanding the panorama-city to the domain of lived experience. Especially in the case of well-known landmarks, which already have a host of visual representations, drawings, photographs, and postcards that celebrate the architectural form, film can provide a critical take on the space. Films that take architecture as their subjects are not mere replications of the built space; they expand upon the physical world and communicate the relationship between community and building, and, in the case of the films analysed here, they make visible the public debates and intimate grievances that are housed within these developments.

Notes

[1] All translations are our own.

[2] After Frank Gehry's construction of the Bilbao Guggenheim Museum was completed in 1997, the former industrial city of Bilbao suddenly became a popular tourist destination and hotspot for other spectacular architectural projects. This effect which star architects (hence the term, 'starchitect') and iconic architecture can have on place-making and the urban development of a city has since been termed 'the Bilbao Effect' (McNeill, 2009: 81).

[3] Mixing archive footage and documentary footage in the style of a film essay, *Bye Bye Malmö* documents the dismantling of the Kockums crane and loss of a landmark for a whole community. The crane was dismantled in 1997 after the demise of Malmö's shipbuilding industry and sold to South Korea for US$1 (Cho 2007).

[4] The film was also funded and supported by the following groups: RTVV Valencia (Spain), TV Ontario (Canada), YLE Teema (Finland), NPS (The Netherlands), ORF (Australia), ETV (Estonia) and The Media Program of the European Union (MEDIA).

Works Cited

Bye Bye Malmö. Dir. Fredrik Gertten. WG Film, 2002.

Cho, Kyung Bok. 'Korean Shipbuilders Hold Off China on Pricier Orders.' *Bloomberg* 8 May 2007. 7 Jan. 2014. <http://www.bloomberg.com/apps/news?pid=21070001&sid=aDm.5.mEHJnU>

De Certeau, Michel. *The Practice of Everyday Life*. Berkeley and Los Angeles, California: University of Califoria Press, 1997.

Eskilsson, Lena and Elisabeth Högdahl. 'Cultural Heritage across Borders? – Framing and Challenging the Snapphane Story in Southern Sweden.' *Scandinavian Journal of Hospitality and Tourism* 9.1, 2009, 65-80.

Eteläpää, Heikki. 'Leski on labiili.' *Uusi Suomi*. 21 Jan. 1968.

Goldberger, Paul. 'The Sculptor.' *The New Yorker*. Condé Nast, 31 Oct. 2005. 14 Oct. 2013. http://www.newyorker.com/archive/2005/10/31/051031crsk_skyline

Guide: Western Harbour. Sustainable City Development. Malmö: Malmö Stad - Environmental Department, 2009.

Jansson, Andre. 'Re-encoding the Spectacle: Urban Fatefulness and Mediated Stigmatisation in the "City of Tomorrow".' *Urban Studies* 42.10, 2005, 1671–1691.

Kääpä, Pietari. *World Film Locations*: Helsinki. Bristol: Intellect, 2013.

Luoma, Matti. '...ainakin yhden keskustelun arvoinen.' *Aamulehti*. 28 Jan. 1968.

Löfgren, Orvar. 'Moving Metaphors.' *Invoking a Transnational Metropolis: The Making of the Øresund Region*. Eds Per Olof Berg, Anders Linde-Laursen, and Orvar Löfgren. Lund: Studentlitteratur, 2000, 27–54.

McNeill, Donald. *The Global Architect: Firms, Fame and Urban Form*. New York; London: Routledge, 2009.

Meurman, Otto I. *Asemakaavaoppi*. Helsinki: Otava, 1954.

Miettinen, Irmeli. 'Tunnetteko te vihreitä leskiä?' *Uusi Maailma* 3.68, 1968, 29.

Salokorpi, Asko. *Modern Architecture in Finland*. London: Weldenfeld & Nicolson, 1970.

Sossen, arkitekten och det skruvade huset. Dir. Fredrik Gertten. WG Film, 2005.

Standertskjöld, Elina. *Arkkitehtuurimme Vuosikymmenet: 1960-1980*. Helsinki: Rakennustieto Oy, 2011.

Talvi, Jussi. 'Vihreät aviomiehet.' *Uusi Maailma* 3.68, 1968, 13.

Toiviainen, Sakari. *Uusi suomalainen elokuva*. Helsinki: Otava, 1975.

Tryggestad, Kjell and Susse Georg. 'How objects shape logics in construction.' *Culture and Organization* 17.3, 2001, 181-197.

Tuomikoski, Eero. 'Vihreä Leski.' *Aamulehti*. 30 Jan. 1968.

Vihreä Leski. Dir. Jaakko Pakkasvirta. Filminor, 1968.

von Hertzen, Heikki. *Koti vaiko kasarmi lapsillemme*. Helsinki: WSOY, 1946.

von Hertzen, Heikki. *Raportti Kaupungin Rakentamisesta: Tapiolan arkea ja juhlaa*. Espoo: Länsiväylä Oy, 1984.

Yksityisalue. Dir. Maunu Kurkvaara. Kurkvaara-Filmi, 1962.

The Horse and his Hero: A Symbiotic Relationship in Old Norse Literature

Harriet Jean Evans
University of York

While scholars have discussed the hero time and again in relation to Old Norse sources, limited attention has been given to the function of the horse in these heroic narratives. Such anthropocentrism seems misguided, as continuing studies in other disciplines suggest animals contribute to the shaping of personal identities and social consciousness, acting, consequently, as a mirror of human behaviour and abilities (Jennbert, 2011; Shepherd, 1996). Named and treated as 'quasi human', the horse's prominent position in early societies has naturally given the horse a prominent position in myths, legends, and heroic traditions (Hurn, 2012; Başgög, 1993). This paper examines the presentation of horses and their interaction with heroes in the heroic poetry of the Old Norse tradition.

Although most famously revered for their seafaring skills, the peoples of the Scandinavian medieval period were also accomplished horsemen (Miller, 2010). Horses are common in the Scandinavian archaeological record, and Viking Age representations of horses and horsemen are found on jewellery, brooches, armour, textiles, and picture stones, suggesting the well-trained horse was an important part of life (Jennbert, 2011). This is reflected in medieval literary sources, as individualised, named horses appear in both skaldic and eddic poetry. The most famous horse in the Scandinavian heroic tradition is Grani, the horse of Sigurðr Fáfnisbani, and this paper is specifically concerned with the relationship between the horse and the hero as presented in the Sigurðr-cycle from the *Poetic Edda*. This paper will first examine the role of Grani in the death of Sigurðr (his hero), and then discuss how both Sigurðr and gold are presented as the burden of Grani. Both these aspects of the horse-hero relationship are part of a general trend in heroic eddic poetry, in which gold and horses are linked and used as indicators of a hero's worth. The heroic poetry of the *Poetic Edda* provides a landscape of mountains and *myrkviðr* (mirkwood), through which heroes ride to adventure and battle. In this world of honour and death, with brief moments of love in between, the horse is both a partner to the hero and an important symbol of heroic status. Although the date of the *Poetic Edda* manuscript is fairly late (c.1270), the texts contained within it are considered as written versions of oral traditions, some of which potentially date from the early Viking Age (Kellogg, 1991; de Vries, 1963; Finch, 1993; Ashman Rowe, 2006).

The figures discussed in this paper are Sigurðr Fáfnisbani, his wife Guðrún and her brothers Högni and Gunnarr, and Gunnarr's wife Brynhildr, who is in love with Sigurðr. Grani is Sigurðr's horse, and Fáfnir is a creature slain by Sigurðr, usually identified as a dragon guarding a treasure hoard. References to Helgi and Sigrún refer to characters from the Helgi poems, heroic poems with Scandinavian roots (compared to the probable Germanic origins of the Sigurðr-cycle).

The death of Sigurðr

Sigurðr's death is traditionally brought about by Högni and Gunnarr at the instigation of Brynhildr, Gunnarr's wife. There are various versions of his death, but in all but one example from the *Poetic Edda*, Sigurðr's death cannot be enacted or visualised without the presence of Grani. *Guðrúnarkviða II* (4), which follows the tradition of the hero being killed outside, portrays Grani as the messenger bringing Guðrún news of the hero's death, and this death is visualised through the separation of Grani and Sigurðr.

> Grani rann af þingi, gnýr vas at heyra, en þá Sigurðr sjalfr eigi kom; (Jónsson, 1926: 359)
>
> Grani ran from the assembly, the roar was heard, and then Sigurðr himself did not come;[1]

Grani is presented here as an active presence, while Sigurðr is stationary and no longer able to ride. The emphasis laid on the inactive figure as *Sigurðr / sjalfr* (Sigurðr himself) potentially suggests that Sigurðr and Grani are so often together, that when they are separated, further qualification is needed to remind the audience of the fact. Grani is also described as running *af þingi* (from the assembly); a link can perhaps be made between this specific action and horse-races, which were a common occurrence at assembly sites in pre-Christian northern Europe (Atkin, 1977-78; Solheim, 1956). The term *hestaþing* (meeting for a public horse fight) is used in the later Icelandic sagas, further emphasising the link between horse sports and assemblies (Hoek-Springer, 2000). The horses are also described as sweating in the second half of this stanza, a ritually important state for sacrificial animals, often reached through racing (Jónsson, 1926; Hoek-Springer, 2000). An account of horse sacrifice taking place in a Scandinavian death ritual is recorded in the *Risala* of Ibn Fadlān, an Arab chronicler who was sent on an embassy to the King of the Bulgars in 921 AD. In this account, horses are raced until they are sweating and then killed to be cremated with the dead man. Hoek-Springer describes the episode observed by Ibn Fadlān as a potential 'ritual of purification', as the sweating horses are apparently killed as part of the ritual of cremation (Hoek-Springer, 2000: 27). If such conclusions on sweating and running can be applied to this episode from *Guðrúnarkviða II*, it sets up an intriguing relationship between Sigurðr's death and the ritually purified state of his horse. This section may imply Grani will be accompanying his hero in death as he did in life.

In the poems of the *Poetic Edda*, Grani is portrayed in almost human terms. Stanza 5 of *Guðrúnarkviða II*, attributes Grani with sentimental attachments and an awareness of the machinations of men, as well as the ability to communicate with Guðrún, who perhaps acts as a substitute for the dead Sigurðr. However, this female figure cannot replace Sigurðr, as the poet reminds the audience of Sigurðr's privileged place in Grani's presence by emphasising *eigendr né lifðut* (his master was not living):

> Gekk ek grátandi við Grana rœða, úrughlýra jó frák spjalla, hnipnaði Grani, drap í gras höfði, jór þat vissi, eigendr né lifðut. (Jónsson, 1926: 359)

> I went weeping to converse with Grani; wet-cheeked, I asked the horse for news; Grani became sorrowful, let his head hang down into the grass, the horse knew, that his master was not living.

Guðrún's weeping, doubly emphasised, matches Grani's own act of mourning, of which Eleazar Meletinsky has found parallels in similar scenes from North Russian folk-laments (Meletinsky, 1998). Grani is placed as the confidante of Guðrún, and companion of Sigurðr. This role is especially emphasised in these descriptions of the hero's death.

However, in *Sigurðarkviða hin meiri* (10-11), potentially an earlier example of the Sigurðr legend, the occasion of Sigurðr's death is recounted rather differently:

> Úti stóð Goðrún Gjúkadóttir, ok hón þat orða alls fyrst of kvað hvar 's nú Sigurðr, seggja dróttinn, es frændr mínir fyrri ríða. (Jónsson, 1926: 318)

> Outside stood Guðrún, the daughter of Giuki, and these are the words that first she said: 'Where now is Sigurðr, lord of warriors, when my kinsmen are riding ahead?'

Rather than simply an observation of the displacement of Sigurðr in relation to her brothers, Guðrún's speech shows she is alerted to the death of her husband when she sees her kinsmen *fyrri ríða* (riding ahead). This phrase indicates the relationship between the hero and the act of riding: if he is no longer riding, Guðrún knows Sigurðr is no longer fulfilling his role as *seggja dróttinn* (lord of warriors), and is therefore deceased. In contrast to *Guðrúnarkviða II*, in which Grani is portrayed as interacting with Guðrún, Grani plays no actively present role in this earlier poem: his actions, like the fate of Sigurðr, are entirely related second-hand by Högni. However, such a framework does not diminish Grani's importance in the episode, as Högni must deliver news of Sigurðr and Grani simultaneously:

> Einn því Högni andsvör veitti: sundr höfum Sigurð sverði höggvinn, gnapir æ grár jór of grami dauðum. (Jónsson, 1926: 318-319)

> Only Högni gave an answer: 'asunder we have hewed the head of Sigurðr with a sword, the grey horse bows his head always over the dead prince'.

As Högni describes how he and Gunnarr killed Sigurðr, the news is immediately followed by a description of Grani's response to the act in this poem. The horse and the hero cannot be separated, further emphasising the dependent nature of their poetic existence.

Hoek-Springer sees the absence of an active role for Grani as simply an indication of *Sigurðarkviða hin meiri's* status as the earliest poetic version of the death of Sigurðr, in which the importance of Grani and riding is least developed (Hoek-Springer, 2000). However, this view ignores the close relationship between Grani and Sigurðr, which is evident in the compulsion for Högni to relate their final interaction together, despite the absence of both Sigurðr and Grani from the active narrative. The above analysis also reveals that the importance of riding reflected in *Guðrúnarkviða II* is apparent in Guðrún's response to the sight of her brothers riding without Sigurðr in Sigurðarkviða hin meiri. Sigurðr also cannot be imagined post-death without the presence of Grani. In *Guðrúnarhvöt* (19), Guðrún can only wish for the return of Sigurðr from the dead, if he is returned to the living on the back of his horse (Jónsson, 1926: 430-431). The death and post-death of Sigurðr is impossible to imagine without the act of riding, and the actions of his horse.

The burden of Grani

Grani may be considered a character in these poems, but as a horse he is also considered a beast of burden. He is variously imagined as carrying Sigurðr or the treasure taken from Fáfnir, or both. The association made between Sigurðr and the gold is a pertinent one, as both are objects of great value in the poems. In *Grípisspá* (13), a poem in which the future acts of Sigurðr are laid out in a prophetic form, the hero is told:

> Þú munt finna Fáfnis bœli ok upp taka auð hinn fagra, golli hlœða á Grana bógu; ríðr til Gjúka gramr vígrisinn. (Jónsson, 1926: 273)

> You will find Fáfnir's den and take up the beautiful treasure, load the gold onto Grani's back; ride to Giuki's, the ready-to-do-battle prince.

Here, gold is specifically associated with Grani's back, and the loading of gold is immediately followed by a command for Sigurðr to ride. The killing of Fáfnir and the subsequent taking of treasure is Sigurðr's first and most well-known heroic act, and therefore the gold he loads onto Grani's back is the foundation on which his reputation is built. *Oddrúnargrátr* (20) refers to the treasure of Fáfnir as *hliðfarm Grana* (the burden of Grani), and so it seems the act of carrying treasure is one of Grani's primary roles in the legend cycle (Jónsson, 1926: 380).

Sigurðr as the burden of Grani is an image commonly used in descriptions of his worth. His primary status among the heroic cast of these poems is often represented in terms of his superior horse, which is set in contrast to other mounted figures in the texts. Brynhildr's devotion to Sigurðr is also repeatedly represented through the image of him riding Grani. In *Sigurðarkviða hin skamma* (40), Brynhildr reveals:

> Þeim hétumk þá þjóðkonungi, es með golli sat á Grana bógum,
> (Jónsson, 1926: 343)
>
> I betrothed myself to him, king of the people, when he sat with gold on Grani's back,

Here, Sigurðr is the worthiest object of Brynhildr's affections precisely because he is seated on Grani's back (something her husband, Gunnarr, was never able to do), and because he is seated alongside Fáfnir's gold. As well as a literal symbol of wealth, the gold can also act as a representation of Sigurðr's heroic achievements. This can be seen in *Helreið Brynhildar* (12), as Brynhildr justifies her devotion to Sigurðr with the phrase: *Reið góðr Grana / gollmiðlandi* (Jónsson, 1926: 355, the good distributor of gold rode on Grani). While great men are often described as distributing wealth in the Old Norse poetic tradition, the link between the distribution of gold and the riding of Grani echoes the association of horses with gold represented elsewhere in the *Poetic Edda*. It is obviously difficult to suggest any intentional competition between poems here, but it is interesting that *Helgakviða Hundingsbana II* (39) depicts Helgi's horse as 'gold-bridled', and *Oddrúnargrátr* (26) describes the horses of Högni and Gunnarr as *hófgollina* (golden-hoofed; Jónsson, 1926: 262, 382). This association of horses with gold spans the entirety of the heroic eddic corpus and is used to signify the importance of a particular hero.[2]

Horsemanship and the hero

The aspects of the Sigurðr-Grani relationship explored above can be seen as part of a wider concern with horsemanship in these texts. While Sigurðr is portrayed as the perfect horseman, other characters are often compared negatively with the image of Sigurðr mounted on Grani. In *Sigurðarkviða hin meiri* (20), Gunnarr is presented as an incompetent rider, and Brynhildr describes a dream in which he is riding in chains. Such a situation is a result of his betrayal of Sigurðr. Although Gunnarr is still mounted, Brynhildr reinforces his disloyal and ignoble acts through the medium of constrained riding:

> ... en þú gramr riðir glaums andvani, fjötri fatlaðr, í fjanda lið. (Jónsson, 1926: 321)

> ... and you, prince, were riding, bereft of merriment, fettered with shackles within a troop of enemies.

This presentation of Gunnarr is contrasted strongly with descriptions of Sigurðr in later stanzas, where Brynhildr describes the oaths of brotherhood Gunnarr and Sigurðr had sworn together, and calls her husband an oath-breaker, while describing Sigurðr in noble terms:

> Þá reyndi þat, es riðit hafði móðigr á vit mín at biðja, hvé herglötuðr hafði fyrri eiðum haldit við hinn unga gram. (Jónsson, 1926: 322)

> Then that was tested when courageous (Sigurðr) had ridden in order to ask for my hand, how the army-destroyer (Sigurðr) had previously kept his oaths to the young prince (Gunnarr).

Here, Brynhildr describes Sigurðr's loyal actions toward Gunnarr. Sigurðr is a *móðigr* (courageous) rider, and one who keeps his oaths, as opposed to Gunnarr who does not. Correct masculine behaviour is linked with competent riding. If referring to the version of the legend in which Sigurðr rides alone through the fire to retrieve Brynhildr, these lines also remind the audience of the exclusivity of the Sigurðr-Grani relationship. Sigurðr's status as the only figure able to ride Grani through the flames is also referred to in *Helreið Brynhildar* (11). This command of Grani is a vital part of Sigurðr's heroic status.

However, extreme domination of horses is a negative motif in these sources. In Scandinavian heroic tradition, horse names such as *alvarr* (all-cautious), *Tjaldari* (ambler), and *fetmóðr* (pace-tired) suggest that the level of exertion allowed on horses should be a serious consideration for the rider (Evans 2013). Similar *heiti* (poetic synonyms) are also evident from *Hamðismal* (3) where horses are referred to as *gangtömum* (gait-tamed), and *Atlakviða* (33), in which Atli's horse is referred to as *eyrskáan* (gravel-pacing) (Jónsson, 1926: 394, 433). In *Guðrúnarkviða II*, the second half of the fourth stanza describes the exertion of the horses of Högni and Gunnarr:

> ... öll váru söðuldýr sveita stokkinn, of vanið vási, und vegöndum. (Jónsson, 1926: 359)

> ... all the saddle-animals were splattered with sweat, accustomed to labours beneath the slayers.

This description has negative connotations, as Högni and Gunnarr are referred to as *vegöndum* (slayers), rather than warriors (Cleasby and Guðbrandur Vigfússon, 1957). That the horses are also described as being accustomed to their labours, perhaps suggests that Högni and Gunnarr routinely over-exert their horses.

Another of the eddic poems from outside of the Sigurðr-cycle, *Helgakviða Hjörvarðssonar* (5.1-4), displays this motif of horses forced to excessively exert themselves in a description of a failed mission. Here, Atli, son of Jarl Iðmundr, and his men have been instructed to retrieve a woman for King Hjörvarðr, but are unable to obtain her:

> Höfum erfiði ok ekki ørendi; mara þraut óra á meginfjalli,
> (Jónsson, 1926: 236)

> We have had trouble and not (achieved) our errand; exhausted (/failed) our horses on high mountains.

Here exhaustion is associated with failure and humiliation, both for the horse and for the hero. Atli and his men have not been able to win the desired woman for their leader, and so they have forced their horses to labour in vain, just as the slayers' horses in *Guðrúnarkviða II* have been forced to exert themselves.

The wording of this stanza potentially supports the idea of the horse as a symbol representing the heroic achievements of the riders: by failing the mission they have also reduced their heroic value. As demonstrated above, horses are often associated with gold in these poems. This association with gold may act as an indication of a hero's worth, and the concept of Fáfnir's treasure, as previously mentioned, is traditionally carried by Grani, and acts as a symbol of Sigurðr's primary heroic achievement. This treasure-taking story may be the source of this association of gold with heroic achievement, and heroic achievement with horses. Inversely, the inability to ride or to control one's horse is often placed alongside failure or betrayal. Gunnarr is unable to control his horse in Brynhildr's dream because he has betrayed Sigurðr; and outside of the Sigurðr-cycle, Sigrún curses her brother's horsemanship because he has betrayed Helgi (Jónsson, 1926: 260). Helgi and Sigurðr are, on the other hand, ideal horsemen, defined by their superior horses, and their superior horsemanship.

Respect for horsemanship, and the interdependent honour-bond of the horse and hero explored above, are recognised and subverted in *Helgakviða Hundingsbana I* (44). In this extract, two men are taking part in a *flyting* (exchange of insults), in which one accuses the other of having been sexually used by Grani:

> Þú vast brúðr Grana á Brávelli, gollbitluð vast gör til rásar, hafðak þór móðri mart skeið riðits svangri und söðli, simul, forbergis. (Jónsson, 1926: 228)

> You were a bride of Grani on Bravoll Plain, were gold-bridled, prepared to gallop; I have ridden you weary on many a downhill stretch of road, lean beneath my saddle, cow.

While the primary purpose of this passage is the identification of the insulted man with a mare – a common and long-lived insult in Old Norse literature – the inclusion of the gold bridle and the repetition of adjectives indicating exhaustion: *svangr* (lean, exhausted) and *móðr* (weary) suggests this insult also alludes to the interaction between the horse and his hero, as discussed in this paper (Clark, 2013; La Farge and Tucker, 1992). It is also interesting that Grani, the greatest legendary stallion, is the figure sexually dominating the mare-figure.

The evidence presented in this paper suggests that the horses in these episodes can be used to define heroic actions and character, distinguish heroic men from their peers, and contribute to the development and self-definition of the hero. Although cases of horses mourning the deaths of their riders is apparent in North Russian folk-laments, these works do not convey the interdependent relationship of the horse and rider as displayed in the Sigurðr-cycle. Unlike Hoek-Springer's suggestion that the importance of Grani in the eddic poems developed over time, the analysis presented in this paper suggests that the importance of horses to the heroes in these poems is present from the earliest poetic incarnations of the legends. Possession of the horse by the hero is vitally important to his heroic status, and lack of control of one's horse is viewed as indicative of failure or failure of one's noble reputation. The masculinity and honour of the hero is always at stake in these narratives, and the hero's horse acts as an effective symbol of his achievements and heroic value, through the association with gold and treasure.

Notes

[1] This, and all other translations, are mine unless otherwise stated.

[2] Although the prose extracts in the *Poetic Edda* are of less evidential value than the poetry, having been added to the corpus at a later date, the relationship between gold and riding is explictly referred to in the prose section added at the end of Fáfnismál, a poem dealing with the slaying of Fáfnir by Sigurðr. This extract describes how Sigurðr loads Grani with the gold taken from the creature, but Grani will not – or cannot – move

until Sigurðr steig á bak hánum (Jónsson, 1926: 305, climbed onto his back). This episode reflects the later view of an established tradition of Grani's exclusivity to Sigurðr, the close relationship between the two, and also the association of Grani with gold, which is repeated in kennings and Viking Age iconography (cf. Hoek-Springer, 2000).

[3] Icelandic authors are noted with their forenames first.

Works Cited[3]

Atkin, Mary. 'Viking Race-Courses? The Distribution of Skeið Place-Name Elements in Northern England.' *Journal of the English Place-Name Society* 10, (1977-78): 26-39.

Başgög, İlhan. 'Proverb Image, Proverb Message, and Social Change.' *Journal of Folklore Research* 30.2/3 (1993): 127-142.

Clark, David. 'Heroic Homosociality and Homophobia in the Helgi Poems.' *Revisiting the Poetic Edda: Essays on Old Norse Heroic Legend.* Eds Paul Acker and Carolyne Larrington. New York and London: Routledge, 2013. 11-27.

Cleasby, Richard, and Guðbrandur Vigfússon. *An Icelandic-English Dictionary*. Oxford: Clarendon Press, 1957.

Evans, Harriet Jean. 'The Horse and his Hero in Old Norse Literature.' Diss. University of York, 2013.

Finch, R. G. '*Atlakviða*.' *Medieval Scandinavia: An Encyclopaedia*. Ed. Phillip Pulsiano. New York: Garland, 1993.

Finnur Jónsson, Ed. *Sæmundar-Edda*. Reykjavík: Kostnaðarmaður Sigurður Kristjánsson, 1926.

Hurn, Samantha. *Humans and Other Animals: Cross-Cultural Perspectives on Human-Animal Interactions.* London: Pluto Press, 2012.

Jennbert, Kristina. *Animals and Humans: Recurrent Symbiosis in Archaeology and Old Norse Religion.* Trans. Alan Crozier. Lund: Nordic Academic Press, 2011.

Kellogg, Robert. 'Literacy and Orality in the Poetic Edda.' *Vox Intexta: Orality and Textuality in the Middle Ages.* Eds Alger Nicolaus Doane and Carol Braun Pasternack. Madison: University of Wisconsin Press, 1991. 89-101.

La Farge, Beatrice, and John Tucker, Eds. *Glossary to the Poetic Edda.* Heidelberg: Carl Winter Universitätsverlag, 1992.

Meletinsky, Eleazar M. *The Elder Edda and Early Forms of the Epic.* Trans. Kenneth H. Ober. Trieste: Edizioni Parnaso, 1998.

Miller, Andrea L. 'Violent Vikings, Gentle Horsemen: The Horse Culture and Practice of Horsemanship in Viking Age Scandinavia.' Diss. Pennsylvania State University, 2010.

Rowe, Elizabeth Ashman. 'Quid Sigvardus cum Christo? Moral Interpretations of Sigurðr Fáfnisbani in Old Norse Literature.' *Viking and Medieval Scandinavia* 2, 2006, 167-200.

Shepherd, Paul. Traces of an Omnivore. Washington D.C.: Island Press, 1996.

Solheim, Svale. *Horse-Fight and Horse-Race in Norse Tradition.* Oslo: H. Aschehoug, 1956.

van der Hoek-Springer, Sarah E. 'Horses in the Viking Imagination.'

Diss. University of Nottingham, 2000.

Vries, Jan de. *Heroic Song and Heroic Legend*. Trans. B.J. Timmer. London: Oxford University Press, 1963.

Anthony Knipe: A Case Study of English Experience in Seventeenth Century Scandinavia

Adam Grimshaw
University of St Andrews

Anthony Knipe emerged from obscurity in 1631 as a merchant and councillor in the city of Gothenburg where he was employed until 1643. Following a fall from favour in Sweden in 1647, Knipe moved to Norway where he was employed in the service of the Danish crown as Customs Officer General from 1649-1654. Once again, Knipe lost his position and was forced to return to England. Despite being marred by near constant controversy, Knipe had a successful career that is worthy of investigation. For the historian, Knipe provides an interesting, if not unique, example of an Englishman's experience in Scandinavia in this period. While a merchant, Knipe held positions of high standing under both the Danish and Swedish crowns and, as a result, associated with influential individuals. In spite of this, exact details of his career and his correspondents are unclear and further investigation is required to provide a full account of his life.

This paper provides a brief insight into the experience of Anthony Knipe during his time in Scandinavia. It initially provides background information regarding English and Scottish commercial activity in northern Europe before moving on to discuss Knipe's career and his role as an emigré in Gothenburg and Bergen. The paper then concludes with questions for further research.

What follows draws on archival sources from the national archives of Sweden and Norway as well as other printed primary sources. A small amount of these sources have been given short treatments in publications relating to the town histories of Gothenburg and Bergen (Almquist, 1929; Fossen, 1979). This is the first time, however, that Knipe's personal correspondence in Sweden has been taken into consideration and a more complete bibliography of his time in Scandinavia has been compiled (SRA, Oxenstierna samlingen).[1] Short entries on Knipe are included in early editions of the national biographical dictionaries of Sweden and Norway (Wiesener, 1936: 431; Svenska Män och Kvinnor, 1948). However, this paper is the first to weave together these disconnected treatments of Knipe, to correct their anomalies, and to place Knipe into a wider historical perspective, posing questions relating to various aspects of Anglo-Scandinavian history in this period.

The Eastland Company and the independent Scots: British trade in Northern Europe in the first half of the seventeenth century

Much like trade to the Levant and the East Indies, official English trade to the Baltic and Scandinavia was handled by a monopoly company which received its first royal charter in 1597 (Hinton, 1959). The Eastland Company, as it was named, aimed to regulate all English trade to and in its designated areas. The company provided protection for its merchants and assisted in cases of piracy or seizure of goods, as well as placing merchant consuls where needed, to help resolve disputes and protect company interests (ibid.).

In contrast, Scottish merchants operating in the same area conducted their trade independently, without the support of a royally sanctioned company. Despite the lack of company protection, Scottish merchants were successful in their trade with Scandinavia and the Baltic. Indeed it has been argued that their independence allowed self-established personal networks to flourish, uninhibited by company rules (Murdoch, 2006). Scottish merchants were more likely than their English counterparts to become burgesses (local member of the merchant community holding specific rights and privileges in order to trade as a native of that region, or possibly even taking citizenship to become a national of the country) of their adopted region (Murdoch, 2006; Åström, 1962). Anthony Knipe however, provides an example of an *English* merchant who obtained burgess status in Sweden and, like his Scottish counterparts, operated independently.

Knipe in Sweden

During the Thirty Years' War, diplomatic relations between the House of Stuart and Sweden were particularly close, due to the notion of a common 'Protestant cause' against the Catholic Habsburg forces of Austria and Spain (Grosjean, 2003). The balance of this relationship, however, overwhelmingly favoured the Scottish Stuarts. This was due to two factors. When James VI acceded to the throne of England to become James VI & I, he ensured there would be only one, united, body of diplomats to represent him and, in the main, ordered the Scottish ambassadors he knew and trusted to represent all his kingdoms (Murdoch, 2003). Furthermore, Scottish migration to Sweden was far more numerous than that of their English counterparts (Grosjean, 2003). Knipe's presence as both an Englishman and independent trader is particularly interesting when set against a backdrop of Scottish migration.

From its foundation in 1621, Gothenburg was designed to encourage foreign migration and settlement. Freedom of religion and trade privileges were used to entice foreign merchants

Methods and Sources

to the region with those of Dutch, Scots, Flemish, and German origin making up the majority, whereas the English were almost negligible in number. The town council itself was intended to represent the foreign make-up of mercantile interest in the city. The town's charter stipulated that four seats should be held by Swedes, three by the Dutch and two seats each to be held by German and Scottish nationals (Andersson, 1996; Grosjean, 2003; Grosjean and Murdoch, 2005; Skarback, 1992).

Knipe is first mentioned in a German Church marriage register in Gothenburg from 1631 (Berg, 1890). In 1635 he acquired the position of *rådsförvant* (city councillor), although at present it is not clear under what nationality he sat, as there was no basis provided for an Englishman to sit on the council as stipulated in the town charter. At the same juncture he was appointed as the head of the city's new English Trading Company in 1635 (RR, 1635: Vol. 189, f. 750; Almquist, 1929).[2] The venture was setup by English and Scottish merchants who intended to make Gothenburg a stable and privileged port for the import of English goods, although merchants from other nations were encouraged to participate (Almquist, 1929). However, the Company was unable to pay the taxes it owed to the Crown throughout 1635 and 1636. This was tolerated, until 1637, when the Company finally folded. Knipe's appointment was criticised by high-ranking councillor Peder Eriksson Rosensköld, as he had not invested any of his own finances in the project, and with the Company's fall Knipe turned on it immediately (Almquist, 1929). The Crown subsequently ordered that the money owed to the Company was to be paid directly to Knipe as a salary for his role as president of the short-lived venture (RR, 1640: Vol. 201, ff. 288-9; Almquist, 1929).[3] It is an early example of how Knipe was able to profit when others fell – a feature of much of his career.

In 1639 Knipe benefited from a nationwide reform of government which named him as Trade President the following year, a position he held until 1643 (RR, 1640: Vol. 201, ff. 313-4; Almquist, 1929).[4] During this time Knipe was influential in the directing and creation of trade policy. In 1639, under the impetus of the Swedish Chancellor Axel Oxenstierna (1612-54), Knipe aided the formulation of rules and regulations relating to the timber mast trade, with a mast inspector appointed in 1642 as a result of his suggestions (Almquist, 1929; SRP, 1639). As a result of the responsibilities of his new position, Knipe travelled to the capital Stockholm on occasion and represented Gothenburg at the *Riksdag* (Swedish Council of State) alongside *burggreve* (Chief Legal Military Officer), Daniel Lange at Nyköping in 1640 (SRP, 1640-41; Almquist, 1929).

As a result of his new position as Trade President, Knipe was in correspondence with the Queen Kristina's Council in regards to Gothenburg and its government. Knipe was also in regular communication with Chancellor Oxenstierna. Such influential correspondents provided Knipe with assistance both professionally, and in aiding more personal disputes (SRA, Oxenstierna samlingen). Unfortunately there are, at present, no known trade statistics or customs records directly linking Knipe to trade. It is through Knipe's correspondence with Oxenstierna it becomes clear that Knipe was involved in the timber trade. According to his own letters he was the eighth largest mast dealer in the city and rented a harbour on the south banks of the city for the final production and export of masts (Almquist, 1929).

As has already been noted in regards to his involvement with the English Trading Company, Knipe could be ruthless in his attempts to ensure his own gain, which resulted in a number of disputes. Knipe argued with his fellow councillors in Gothenburg, incurred large debts to merchants in Stockholm and even maintained a long-standing, public feud with his stepson. For all their flavour and intrigue, there are simply too many disputes to cover them all in such a limited survey. Ultimately, despite Knipe's talent, it was his attitude and personality that eventually led to his downfall in Sweden. He lost support from the influential circles he had mysteriously been able to penetrate, and was expelled from Sweden in 1649. He quickly switched Sweden for Norway and was to repeat many of the same mistakes.

Knipe in Norway

While British relations were generally favourable with Sweden, there was in fact no official alliance until Cromwell's time. However, Britain's relationship with Denmark-Norway was officially represented through the dynastic alliance and marriage of James VI to Christian IV of Denmark's sister Anna in 1589. This alliance was tested, particularly during the reigns of Charles I and Cromwell, but remained intact. As with Sweden, Scots dominated diplomatic affairs with Denmark-Norway until the 1650s (Murdoch, 2003; Murdoch, 2006; Østby-Pedersen, 2005). Again Scottish migration and trade to Norway was far more numerous than English connections with the area (Sogner, 2003; Østby-Pedersen, 2005; Hinton, 1959).

Perhaps anticipating his fall from favour in Sweden and, seeking employment in the dual kingdom of Denmark-Norway, Knipe wrote to the Viceroy of Norway, Hannibal Sehested, in June 1647 (SESR, 1905). Continued correspondence resulted in his appointment as toll commissioner for Norway on 28 July 1649 and Knipe duly moved with his family to Bergen (SESR, 1905; Wiesener, 1936). Knipe was the only man to have held this post, which was possibly created as a result of Hannibal Sehested's tax reforms, which were intended to provide funds for the Crown and pay for military action against Sweden (Rian, 1999; Rian,

2000). It is unclear why Knipe was appointed to this position. It is possible that his reputation preceded him in two different, yet opposing ways. On the one hand he may have been appointed as Danish officials recognised his experience in Gothenburg's trade and government. On the other hand, Sehested may have been aware that his reforms would prove unpopular and desired a scapegoat. As a divisive and turbulent figure, Knipe could easily have fulfilled this role.

From his base in Bergen, Knipe was in charge of ensuring that customs tolls in all Norwegian ports were recorded, paid and shipped to Copenhagen. Knipe's enforcement of customs duties was rigorous from the outset and almost immediately caused a major upset among the city's mercantile community, as well as in local and national government circles. Sources from late 1649 and early 1650 demonstrate how Knipe's method of collecting customs on a ship's immediate arrival in port had alienated the influential Bergen merchants. It had previously been law to collect customs duties at the end of the trade cycle, when local merchants and visiting traders had settled their business. The new method produced a serious cash shortage and forced local merchants to sell their goods at much lower rates, or to enter into unfavourable credit agreements to ruinous consequences (NRA, 1650: litra T T; Fossen, 1979).[5] By 1652 their relationship had deteriorated so badly that the king forced both parties to enter into a treaty aimed at a truce (NRR, Vol. 10, 352).[6] Although a pragmatist, it is likely that the turbulence Knipe encountered was in part due to the sheer magnitude of his task. We can also certainly attribute his disagreeable disposition and ruthlessness as an enforcer of government directives as contributing factors.

Knipe also fell out of favour with his patron Sehested. The reasons for this remain unclear, although Knipe's general personal manner was probably a factor. Fredrik III, however, was so pleased with Knipe that in September 1650, he offered him a lifetime position in his current role, with Viceroy Sehested soon falling out of favour (NRR, Vol. 10, 1887).7 As a customs officer it is not clear if Knipe was entitled to a share of the goods he seized, although his potentially illegal engagement in such activities may provide a likely reason for Sehested's suspicion and disapproval (ibid.).8 Records show that Knipe did not always act within the law in regards to some seizures, while his actions in regard to dispensing justice were particularly questionable.

Mirroring his experience in Sweden, Knipe was becoming increasingly problematic for the Danish administration. The Danish Privy Council questioned his appointment and accused Knipe of embezzlement, stating how it would be too easy for this 'unknown and nefarious man' to escape to Britain with Norway's customs revenue (Wiesener, 1936: 431; Mellbye, 1977-1982: 108).9 There were also accusations that he fathered an illegitimate child while away on business, which was undoubtedly used to further tarnish his reputation (NRR, Vol. 11, 1890).10 Knipe was dismissed from his position in June 1654 and returned to England where he moved into relative obscurity (ibid.; Wiesener, 1936).11

Knipe and Community

As an Englishman, Knipe's presence in Scandinavia is interesting in relation to the foreign societies he operated within. His nationality and position draws further questions when it is acknowledged that he was an Englishman among a British emigrant population in Scandinavia that was predominantly Scottish.

It is currently unclear as to what extent he was involved with the British merchant communities in Bergen and Gothenburg, although the example of the English Trading Company in

Gothenburg does show he was in some form of contact with other English and Scottish merchants in the city. Furthermore, the seizure of Dutch goods in Bergen and the reselling of them to English merchants may hint at possible favour shown to his countrymen. At the very least, it shows that he was in contact with the English during his time in Norway (NRA, 1650: litra Æ Æ; NRR, Vol. 10, 1887).[12] However, his marriage to Maria Langer suggests that he also had direct ties with the wider European community in Gothenburg. Langer, whom Knipe married in 1631, was the daughter of a merchant from the Low Countries. The marriage, at least to some extent, was probably entered into for practical purposes, and it raises further questions of Knipe's involvement with other nationalities in Scandinavia, which still remain to be investigated.

In contrast to the rest of his countrymen, Knipe attained high status during his career in Scandinavia, a feat normally only reserved to Scotsmen of noble background. Knipe's colourful story allows a glimpse into the life of a foreign emigrant to Scandinavia in this period, and raises questions surrounding commercial history, as well as migration and diaspora studies. More research needs to be undertaken to discover how indicative Knipe's activity was of English merchants in Scandinavia during this period. Whether, and to what extent the English interacted with their Scottish counterparts in Scandinavia also needs to be established. Furthermore, Knipe demonstrates the need for a reappraisal when viewing the associations of England with both Sweden and Norway in this period. Our understanding of the trade between England and Scandinavia in this period is still very limited. There was a presence of Englishmen such as Knipe, scattered in towns throughout Scandinavia and the Baltic, acting in some form of commercial capacity. As a high-ranking individual, investigating Knipe's commercial activity, as well as his network of contacts, will hopefully allow for a greater comprehension of how trade was conducted at ground level, and enable us to view the commercial role of these emigrés in their host countries. As Knipe's case makes clear, Scandinavia was open for business and ruthless men like Knipe were ready to exploit every opportunity.

Notes

[1] There exist some 72 separate documents between Oxenstierna, Knipe and Knipe's wife Maria Langer, as well as other related documents. These documents detail Knipe's activities and disputes, as well as his relationships with prominent councillors, merchants and nobility, i.e. decision-makers in Sweden.

[2] Queen Kristina to Gothenburg Town Council concerning establishment of the English Company of Gothenburg and the raising of Anthony Knipe to the Town Council, Stockholm, 18 August 1635.

[3] Donation for Anthony Knipe, Nyköping, 12 March 1640.

[4] Queen Kristina to Gothenburg Town Council, Nyköping, 16 March 1640.

[5] Complaints from the merchants in Bergen with a statement from Anthony Knipe to Fredrik III, April 1650.

[6] Ove Bjelke's letter concerning a treaty between Anthony Knipe and the Bergen burgess community, Copenhagen, 2 January 1652.

[7] Knipe's confirmation of his salary and position, Copenhagen, 11 September 1650.

[8] Knipe's actual salary was stipulated at 5% of the total percentage of tolls taken in Norway. This was granted by the king on 11 September 1650, in tandem with Knipe's confirmation of tenure in his customs role.

[9] [fremmede karl som var infam], my translation into English from Danish.

[10] Jørgen Bielke concerning Anthony Knipe's illegitimate child in Agdesiden, Flensborgshuus, 11 November 1654.

[11] Termination of Customs Officer General Anthony Knipe [eftersom du for adskilligt er beskyldt, hvorfor du deg ennu ikke så nøigatig, som det sig burde], Koldingshuus, 21 June 1654. A travel pass was issued to Knipe for travel through Germany and Holland to England.

[12] 'Relating to Christopher Orning's confiscated ship', 11 October 1649 to 1 February 1650; Two Englishmen receive insurance on a ship sold to them by Anthony Knipe, Copenhagen, 7 June 1650.

Works Cited

Almquist, Helge. *Göteborgs historia: grundläggningen och de första hundra åren.* Göteborg, 1929.

Andersson, Bertil. *Göteborgs historia: näringsliv och samhällsutveckling.* Stockholm, Nerenius & Santérus, 1996.

Berg, Wilhelm. *Samlingar till Göteborgs historia. 3, Christina kyrkas böcker för vigda, födda och döda.* Göteborg, 1890.

Fossen, A. B. *Bergen bys historie.* Vol. 2, Bergen: Universitetsforlaget, 1979.

Grosjean, Alexia. *An Unofficial Alliance.* Leiden: Boston, Brill, 2003.

Grosjean, Alexia and Murdoch, Steve. 'The Scottish Community in Seventeenth-Century Gothenburg.' Grosjean, Alexia and Murdoch, Steve, Eds. *Scottish Communities Abroad in the Early Modern Period.* Leiden: Boston, Brill, 2005, 191-224.

Hinton, R. W. K. *The Eastland Trade and the Common Weal in the Seventeenth Century.* Cambridge: Cambridge University Press, 1959.

Svenska Män och Kvinnor. Vol. 4, 'Knipe, Anthony.' Stockholm: Albert Bonniers Förlag, 1948, 295.

Melbye, Osvald. *Tollere gjennom 300 år, 1563-1886*. Oslo: Norsk Sleksthistorisk Forening, 1977-1982, 108.

Murdoch, Steve. *Britain, Denmark-Norway and the House of Stuart, 1603-1660: A Diplomatic and Military Analysis*. East Linton: Tuckwell Press, 2003.

Murdoch, Steve. *Network North: Scottish Kin, Commercial and Covert Association in Northern Europe, 1603-1746*. Leiden, Boston: Brill, 2006.

Nielsen, Yngvar and Thomle, E. A., Eds. *Norske Rigsregistranter [NRR]*. Vols. 10-11, Christiania: Det Mallingske Bogtrykkeri, 1887-1890.

Norsk Riksarkivet (The National Archives of Norway) [NRA]. Danske Kancelli, skap 14, pakke 344.

Rian, Øystein. 'Sehested, Hannibal.' *Norsk biografisk leksikon [NBL]*. VIII, Oslo: Kunnskapsforlaget, 1999, 148-9.

Rian, Øystein. 'State, Elite and Peasant Power in a Norwegian Region: Bratsberg County in the Seventeenth Century.' [Trans. Per Kristian Halle.] Leon Jespersen, Ed. *A Revolution from Above? The Power State of 16th and 17th Century Scandinavia*. Odense: Odense University Press, 2000, 187-247.

Skarback, Sören. *Göteborg på 1600-talet*. Göteborg: Tre Böcker, 1992.

Sogner, Sølvi. 'Hollandertid og Skottetid.' Knut Kjelstadli Ed., *Norsk innvandringshistorie: i kongenes tid, 900-1814*. Oslo: Pax Forlag A/S, 2003, pp. 293-303.

---. 'Opp fra Danmark: Hertugdømmene og det tyske riket.' Knut Kjelstadli, Ed. *Norsk innvandringshistorie: i kongenes tid, 900-1814*. Oslo, Pax Forlag A/S, 2003, 304-315.

SRA. *Riksregistraturet*. 1112.1/B, Vols. 189 and 201, 1635 and 1640. *Statholderskabets Ekstrakprotokol af Supplicationer og Resolutioner [SESR]*. 1642-1652, Vol. 2, Christiania: J. Chr. Gundersens Bogtrykkeri, 1905.

Svenska Riksarkivet (The National Archives of Sweden) [SRA]. Oxenstierna samlingen, E636.

Svenska Riksrådets Protokoll [SRP]. Vols. 7-8, 1639-1641. Kungl. Boktryckeriet, 1895-8.

Wiesener, A. M. 'Anthony Knipe.' *NBL.* VII. Oslo, Aschehoug, 1936, p. 431.

Åström, S. E. *From Stockholm to St Petersburg.* Helsinki: Finnish Historical Society, 1962.

Østby-Pedersen, Nina. 'Scottish Immigration to Bergen in the Sixteenth and Seventeenth Centuries.' Grosjean, Alexia and Murdoch, Steve. *Scottish Communities Abroad in the Early Modern Period.* Leiden, Boston: Brill, 2005, 135-168.

Chancellor Oxenstierna's War 1635-1643: A Guide to Archival Sources

Björn Nordgren
University of St Andrews

The Thirty Years' War, which engulfed the lands of the Holy Roman Empire between 1618 and 1648, is understood as one of the most destructive conflicts in human history. Unsurprisingly, historians have devoted significant attention to it and produced a plethora of literature on the subject, with varied focuses. The Swedish intervention between 1630 and 1648 is certainly no different in this regard, with a number of books having been written both in English and Swedish. Whilst such a multiplicity of literature should only be viewed through a positive lens, there are nonetheless omissions in the literature that must be addressed. Swedish sources tend to focus narrowly on either King Gustav II Adolf's (1594-1632) foray into the Holy Roman Empire (1630-1632) and the Peace of Westphalia in 1648, whilst the more international literature tends not to make use of the wide array of sources available to an historian of the Swedish conflict. Thus, this article seeks to engage with these two particular areas of neglect, which are prevalent in the literature on the Thirty Years' War. The first question is of periodisation, which is essential to engage with, given the length of the conflict, but which has inevitably caused some problems. The second question, more specific to the Swedish historian, is of sources, for although an extensive literature does exist, surprisingly few works actually interact with the large source base that is available both in printed form and in the Swedish archives.

In order to achieve these aims, this paper is structured in two sections. The first section presents how the war has been divided into different 'periods' in previous literature, then continues to argue for a further division of the neglected second period of the conflict (1635-1648). The second section deals more specifically with the sources that are available to Swedish historians, and how they can be engaged with for use in the historical record. The article ends with a summary discussion in which some conclusions are made as to the impact this will make on the existing literature.

Periodisation

We shall thus begin with the question of periodisation, a question which is often taken as a given but rarely discussed in a nuanced way. Indeed, this is important because the thirty-year period is too unwieldy for discussion. The division of the conflict into five distinct phases has ostensibly solved this problem and can be outlined thus:

1) 1618-21: The Bohemian Revolt
2) 1621-25: The Palatinate phase
3) 1625-29: The Danish Intermezzo
4) 1630-35: The Swedish phase
5) 1635-48: The Swedish-French phase

This model of five distinct phases may be overly simplistic. It gives the impression that the stages of war were in some way static or clear-cut, and does not give an impression that these phases flow into each other. This was of course not true, as the Swedish involvement, for instance, could reasonably be argued as having begun in 1628 with the defence of Stralsund rather than in 1630, as traditional scholarship would suggest. Moreover, it is noticeable that the model is nation-based, with the point at which a new belligerent enters the fray as a division marker. However, this only leaves space for the traditional participants, i.e. the Emperor and the Princes, France, and Sweden, and ignores the less direct belligerents such as the States-General which, whilst not involved directly per se, did contribute significant aid against the Imperial side. Moreover, the Eighty Years' War provided an important diversionary conflict.

This disparity is perhaps forgivable, given that it is, after all, difficult to encompass all belligerents and indeed all aspects of the conflict at a level that would please all historians. However, one further incongruence is created by such time-period divisions: the disparity between the first eighteen years of the conflict (1618-1635) divided into four distinct phases, and the last thirteen (1635-1648), merely sectioned off as one single phase. Such a noticeable temporal disparity is surprising given the level of detail at which the first portion has been dealt with, and even more astonishing given the significance of the later part of the war in our understanding of the Peace of Westphalia and how the terms were reached. A great number of books have mapped the importance of the Peace in its wider historical context, but little has actually been done on how such an important agreement was achieved. Indeed, the question of this lack of coverage for the latter part of the war was first discussed by Gunther Mueller in 1978, and to illustrate his case Mueller uses historians C.V. Wedgwood and Josef Polisensky as examples (Mueller, 1978: D1055-56). Wedgwood devoted 314 pages to the period before 1635 and 112 pages to the period after (Wedgwood, 1968), the same numbers for Polisensky are 216 and 50 pages (Polisensky, 1971). This disproportionality was also evident in further examples that Mueller provided. The best modern treatment of the Thirty Years' War, *Europe's Tragedy* by Peter H. Wilson (2009), does not have this problem and instead seeks to address it directly. At 997 pages long however, Wilson's ambitious tome is not the most accessible piece of work and is perhaps an argument in itself as to why historians adopted the system of phases in the first place. Furthermore, whilst Wilson shows a clearer emphasis on the second part of the war, he does so by highlighting the importance of the French involvement at the expense of the Swedish (Höbelt, 2010). Wilson's book does little to elucidate the actions of Sweden during the period and thus an important belligerent at this stage remains under-researched.

A New Model?

By following the progress of the Swedish army in the period after 1635, it is possible to create a more nuanced picture of this period than has been done in previous studies:

a) 1635-37: Treading Water

Although this period contains within it the battle of Wittstock on 24 September 1636 — essential in restoring the reputation of the Swedish army — it was still a case of survival. Immediately following the devastating loss at the battle of Nördlingen in August 1634, the army was at the smallest it had ever been at any stage during the war — 26,000 soldiers — and though it increased to 53,000 by January 1636 (Tingsten, 1932; Ericsson-Wolke, 1998) it remained small in comparison with the Imperial one. Moreover, the battle of Wittstock in September 1636 had taken its toll and being chased by the Imperial army, the army once again found itself isolated to Northern Germany at the end of the period.

b) 1638-39: Recovery

The years 1638-39 were described by Swedish Field-Marshal Johan Banér as the most boring period of the war, but they were also essential for the army's survival. Although no actual figures are available, around 20,000 new recruits from Sweden bolstered the ranks and several levies were held abroad in places like the UK (Tingsten, 1932: 103). At the end of 1639, the army was once again making progress, and made its way into enemy territory.

c)   1640-41: Dip

Despite the renewed effort, the army once again faced trouble. Although the campaign of 1640 was relatively successful, internal relations within the army were far from amicable, and they worsened at the beginning of 1641 with attempts by Banér to coax troops away from French allies. Following the death of the Field Marshal, disagreements with the Swedish government over pay led to twenty-three officers taking the main army leadership hostage and it was only through negotiation that order was restored.

d)   1641-43: Victory?

After the installation of a new Field Marshal and a thorough refocusing of the army leadership to include more of the foreign elements, the army was once again on its feet. The new Field Marshal Lennart Torstensson came with crucial reinforcements, and thus the army once again increased in size. It was by these means Torstensson was able to achieve a vital victory at Leipzig, which facilitated Oxenstierna's invasion of Denmark-Norway.

e)   1644-48: Diplomacy

That the war needed to come to an end was understood as early as 1643. However, it took five years of negotiating and military maneuvering to get to the stage where both parties were in agreement. Moreover, this phase contained the battle of Jankow in 1645, which was recognised not only as an important Swedish victory, but also as a significant chapter in the history of military warfare.

This quick survey of the last portion of the war from the Swedish perspective is simplistic and does not include many facets of research done, but then it is not within the scope of this paper to do this. What it does illustrate, however, is that this phase of the war was a great deal more complex than other histories have claimed and a great deal has therefore been lost by not researching this area. This article will now progress to the second section which will deal with the sources available in the archives and in print for such a study.

The Sources

a)   The Army

For an historian of this period of the war, the Swedish army is a fascinating construct and one which must be engaged with in order to produce an accurate picture of the actions orchestrated. It is difficult to talk of it as just one army on the Swedish side, as often there were two or even three armies in the field at once, as much for practical reasons as it was out of necessity. Nor is it possible to talk of the armies as particularly Swedish. Although the Swedish government controlled the armies, Swedish regiments were in the minority, and the armies were filled with Scottish, English, and German soldiers. One of the reasons why it is possible to ascertain such a fact is because of how well documented the army was, and one of the most important sources in this respect is the Muster Roll.

The Muster Roll was a record of the officers and soldiers present in a regiment at the time of muster, the gathering of soldiers and officers that took place every two to three months. The listing of officers in the roll is done in order of rank, with the commanding officer of the regiment listed first and then all the senior officers after that. This of course provides an important indication of how the regiment was constructed in terms of command. Another point of interest in the roll is also that each individual soldier is recorded, which not only provides an indication of the soldier's path through the Thirty Years' War but can also give an overview of the structure of the regiment in terms of nationality. Here it is absolutely crucial to point out that Sweden is completely unique at this time for having recorded the soldiers in such a manner, and the roll is an invaluable tool. Muster rolls are limited however to the extent that they only provide a picture of the regiments that were present in Sweden or in garrisons in the Empire as this is where they could be mustered. Thus they only indicate the garrisoned troops of an army, and to get assessments of the numbers in the armies in movement one must use reports from either the Field Marshal or Oxenstierna, which, fortunately, are quite numerous.

The Muster Roll is also an example of the means by which Sweden's Krigskollegium (War College), the government body responsible for running all aspects of the army, kept tabs on the regiments in the field. This in turn was part of the wider governmental apparatus which sought centralised control over all facets of state. This was reinforced by the Form of Government in 1634. The War College furthermore kept detailed records of letters received, explaining actions of levying soldiers for regiments, specific farmers that were spared from the levy, or simply recording important news that came from the army in the Empire. These in turn provide an invaluable insight into the day-to-day running of the army, something which historians have mostly failed to acknowledge.

b) Battles

Due to the nature of the conflict and although the War College had control over the actual levying of men in Sweden, the armies in the Empire functioned completely independently of the Swedish state. Preservation of the armies was key and battles were not risked often on account of the human cost being so immense. Historians have therefore questioned the decisive nature of pitch battles and the role they played in the conflict as a whole (Parker, 1997). Be this as it may, Swedish Field Marshals never lost sight of the fact that battles were important, and there were two absolutely crucial events during the period 1635-43. As with most major events there is a great deal written about them, and references are made to the battles in letters. For instance, for Wittstock there were no less than three accounts written: one by Field Marshal Johan Banér (1596-1641), another by Field Marshal Alexander Leslie (1582-1661) and the third by Lieutenant General James King (1589-1652). For Leipzig, in October 1642, there were two. These accounts do not always agree (in fact, in the case of Wittstock they definitely do not), but they nevertheless outline the actions taken by each individual commander during the event and provide historians with a vital insight into how these battles were carried out.

Other sources can be used for corroboration in this instance. Orders of battle were drawn up by the main army commanders the night before a battle, indicating where they intended to place the regiments the following day. These were, it should be pointed out, merely suggestions, but do nonetheless indicate roughly where the regiments were to stand. Indeed, the deviation between these and battle maps drawn up after the event are usually slight, but one needs to study both in order to get the most accurate picture of how the actual event took place. This is crucial, as the portrayal of individuals or actions in battles are an important element of how the war was fought.

c) Diplomacy

Battles and campaigning alone cannot account for the achievement of Sweden's desired aims, and the Treaty of Westphalia was a culmination not only of the fighting but also of five years of feverish diplomatic activity. One important piece of the diplomatic puzzle is the treaties themselves, and the Treaty of Westphalia is found in many different versions around Sweden and elsewhere. The intricate treaty shows not only the signatures of those present, which were hugely important, but also the terms that had been agreed. However, these treaties reveal very little of the actual diplomatic process behind them. In the Swedish case, the diplomatic correspondences sent to and from the negotiators are useful to reinforce this. Here, Oxenstierna's letters are vital, as he was not only the de facto leader of Sweden but also leader of Kansliet (the Chancery), which was responsible for foreign policy and a source for diplomatic activity. If one moves backward in time from Westphalia to the negotiations of the Treaty of Stuhmnsdorf which began in June 1635 and were concluded in September of the same year, the level of control that the Chancellor craved over the whole process is clear. On the surface, the treaty itself reveals an agreement that was expensive for Sweden, and meant that although peace had been bought for another twenty-six years, it had been done so through the loss of Danzig, an important centre for raising tolls and an invaluable financial resource. However, a more detailed look at the correspondence concerning the negotiations, specifically those between the Chancellor and his son Johan Oxenstierna (1611-1657), reveals the Chancellor's frustration with the lack of communication. Oxenstierna, believing Poland to be a more pressing problem than the Emperor, wanted a harder line to be taken, whilst the Swedish council, the Riksråd, wanted quite the opposite. Further correspondence in the wake of the Treaty reveals Axel Oxenstierna's anger at having been sidelined, and that he expected to be kept appraised of government actions. Whilst it is not within the scope of this article to delve any further into this matter, it is important to emphasise that without these sources being used to support each other, the full dimensions of diplomatic discussions cannot be revealed.

Conclusion

Diplomatic letters are an important source for a historian wishing to write about Sweden and the later part of the Thirty Years' War, as are governmental sources and sources pertaining to the management of the army. It is through their combined use that one can fully ascertain the actions and motives behind the continued Swedish war after 1635. What is, of course, unfortunate is the situation that gave birth to the need for such a study in the first place: the 'periodisation conundrum', which has meant that the last portion of the war is under-researched. Indeed, even though more thorough modern research, such as Wilson's, has gone some way towards filling the gap, our understanding of the war is still disappointing with regard to Sweden's participation. This paper has identified the problem and highlighted sources that can aid in addressing it, making the Thirty Years' War historiography a great deal more balanced than it is today.

Works Cited

Ericson-Wolke, Lars. 'Hur Jöran Tomasson kom till Prag 1648: eller en finländare i Trettioåriga Kriget.' *Krig och Krigsmakt under Svensk Stormaktstid*. Lund: Historiska Media, 2004. 189-199.

---. *Vägen till Westfaliska freden: Sverige och trettioåriga kriget*. Lund: Historiska Media, 1998.

Grosjean, Alexia. *An Unofficial Alliance: Scotland and Sweden, 1569-1654*. Leiden: Brill, 2003.

Höbelt, L. Rev of Wilson. 'Europe's Tragedy: A History of the Thirty Years' War.' *Journal of Early Modern History* 14.3, 2010, 285-287.

Mueller, Guenther. 'Thirty Years' War or Fifty Years of War.' *The Journal of Modern History* 50.1, 1978, D1053-D1056.

Parker, Geoffrey, Ed. *The Thirty Years' War*. London: Routledge, 1997.

Polisensky, J.V. *The Thirty Years' War*. Trans. Robert Evans. London: University of California Press, 1971.

Tingsten, Lars. *Fältmarskalkerna Johan Banér and Lennart Torstensson såsom Härförare*. Stockholm: Militärlitteraturföreningens Förlag, 1932.

Wedgwood, C.V, *The Thirty Years' War*. London: Methuen Publishing, 1968.

Wilson, Peter. *Europe's Tragedy: A History of the Thirty Years' War*. London: Penguin, 2009.

Finnish National Identity and the Ingrian Right to Return Law: A Critical Discourse Analysis

Nicholas Prindiville
University College London

From 1990 to 2010, Finland's immigration service (the Maahanmuuttovirasto) followed a policy of preferential treatment and expatiated granting of residency permits for those deemed, according to the service's website, to 'have Finnish ancestry or otherwise a close connection with Finland'. Once an applicant's 'Finnishness' or connection to Finland was proven, 'no other reason, such as work or study, is required in order to receive the permit.' The Maahanmuuttovirasto's website presented this policy as a 'Returnees' program, implying the granting of right to return to Finnish émigrés and their families, yet the website also specifically addresses the eligibility of 'returnees' from the former Soviet Union, noting that 'A person from the former Soviet Union can be granted a residence permit if the person's *nationality* is Finnish, i.e. he or she is not a Finnish *citizen* but is of Finnish origin in terms of ethnic background' (Maahanmuuttovirasto, my translation, emphasis in the original). Here, a problem arises: how exactly should a 'returnee' be defined? Is the term 'returnee' itself bound by the physical act of returning to a region previously inhabited? Or is it a somewhat more loaded term, implying return to a less literal, and more mythical or symbolic homeland that is defined by some form of ethnic kinship? These questions suggest a broader question as to how the national community, and thus the nation itself, is defined through citizenship.

This paper investigates how ethnicity, and an ethnic understanding of identity and citizenship, is reflected in Finland's right to return policy. Finland presents a prime example of a nation-state where the division between nationality and citizenship is grey and murky; Päivi Harinen et al. (2007: 132) note that the Finnish terms for nationality (kansallisuus) and citizenship (kansalaisuus) are 'difficult to distinguish from one another, even etymologically'. They argue that Finnish citizenship policy 'has been flavoured both by national and by ethno-cultural protectionism...[based on] the myth of the cultural, ethnic and religious homogeneity of Finnish society' (ibid.). The use of Finland as a case study to illustrate this intersection between citizenship, ethnicity, and national identity depends on the history of Finland as a contested territory existing between European Great Powers and subject to fluctuating borders and political status. The population of ethnic Finns in the Soviet Union was concentrated in Ingria, a historic region on the easternmost point of the Baltic Sea, surrounding the eastern end of the Gulf of Finland, which historically has served as a borderland between the Russian and Swedish spheres of influence. Prior to its annexation by the Swedish Crown in 1617 at the end of the Ingrian War, this area was a sparsely inhabited outer-region of the Russian province of Novgorod, populated largely by indigenous Baltic peoples (Izhorians and Votes). However, during the course of the seventeenth century, the Swedish kings consolidated Ingria into the greater province of Finland, and the region built up a significant population of émigrés from Finland, making them the dominant ethnic group in the region (Nylund-Oja et al., 1995). This was to change dramatically following the Great Northern War of 1700 – 1721, during which the Russian Tsar Peter the Great reclaimed Ingria and constructed his new capital, St Petersburg in its centre, bringing a dramatic influx of Russians that eventually reduced the Ingrian Finns to a minority population in the region (ibid.). Ingria has remained part of Russia since this reconquest, successively as a part of the Russian

Empire, the Russian Socialist Republic within the Soviet Union, and the modern-day Russian Federation, and today corresponds roughly to the Russian province of Leningrad Oblast, which surrounds the federal city of St Petersburg. However, though Finns were overtaken as the dominant ethnic in the St Petersburg region in the late eighteenth century, they have remained a significant minority group, retaining second position until the 1920s (Rimpiläinen, 2001).

The significance of Ingria as border-region underlines Anssi Paasi's (1996) study of the changing sociological function of the Finnish-Russian frontier; for much of the twentieth century this boundary formed part of the Iron Curtain, separating the Communist East from the Capitalist West as a clear ideological border. However, the collapse of Communism in the late 1980s and early 90s marked the end of this relatively clear separation, and precipitated a rise of 'diverging ethno-regionalistic and ethno-nationalistic movements' as identity and social-grouping processes (ibid.). Thus the role history and geography play in defining (or complicating) identity in border regions has particular resonance for Finland. Likewise, the fact that ethnic groups do not correspond (or indeed may never have corresponded) exactly to nation-states, denotes the limits of a geographical or interfrontier definition of a nation-state, given the impermanence of boundaries, highlighted in the Finnish example.

In this paper, I employ critical discourse analysis (CDA) to analyse how the shifting structural relationship between state and ethnicity, as Finland adapted to the new post-Soviet international relations context of the 1990s and new millennium. CDA is distinguished from alternative discourse analysis methods through its focus on power, and how discursive interpretations are made ideologically dominant by power inequalities (Hjelm, 2011). Ruth Wodak et al. (1999: 8) write that CDA is tasked with unmasking 'ideologically permeated and often obscured structures of power, political control and dominance' in language use. In the Ingrian Finnish case, an ideologically dominant discursive construction of Finnish identity may be created using the power structures that exist within lawmakers' ability to legislate and define identity through citizenship and immigration law. Such a law produces a statement on who is included and excluded within the discursively produced identity parameters that define Finnish national identity. As argued in this paper, the political discourse surrounding the Finnish Right to Return created a reasonably stable construction of Finnish national identity, which was used to first prove, and later disprove, a relationship between Ingrian Finns and the Finnish state.

The Ingrian Right to Return Law

The Ingrian Finnish return law was first proposed in 1990. For Finnish politicians, this was a year of change, a theme that came out in several different public speeches given by ministers of the Finnish government that year. Prior to 1990, Finnish governments had generally followed a line of foreign and defence policy, the so-called Paasikivi-Kekkonen line, which involved strict neutrality and great care to ensure a peaceful relationship with their neighbours to the east, the Soviet Union. But now, with the collapse of the Berlin Wall in late 1989, and the decline of the Soviet Union and Cold War tensions, there was a reassessment of Finland's foreign and defence policy priorities. The then-foreign minister of Finland, Pertti Paasio, gave a speech in Washington DC when the Berlin Wall came down, in which he spoke of the Fall of the Wall as the collapse of the entire Cold War security landscape in Europe, suggesting that now, European nations would be able to assert their concerns and differences without having to cleave to the apparently out-dated notions of the Warsaw Pact, NATO and Neutral blocks.[1]

For historian W.R Mead (1991), one significant change in Finnish politics after the Iron Curtain was raised was the increasing willingness of Finnish politicians to express concern for the welfare of the Finnish-speaking minority in Russia. The key voice that made the Ingrian Finns a special issue for Finland from 1990 was the President of Finland, Mauno Koivisto's. Early that year, he instructed the Finnish Immigration Service, responsible for the issuing of residence permits, to start granting residency to Ingrian Finns as 'return' migrants (Malinen, 1999: 195). This was a special category of residency, granted to those who had been Finnish citizens, but had lost their citizenship by immigrating abroad, as well as their descendants. It was designed mostly to allow those descended from Finnish citizens who had left for North America in the early twentieth century, and particularly those who had moved to Sweden in the mid-twentieth century, to come and live in their former homeland (Kirwan and Harrigan, 1986). This wasn't exactly the case for Ingrians – many had no relatives who had ever been Finnish citizens, since they had been residents of Ingria since before Finland existed as a nation-state. Yet for President Koivisto, there still existed a connection between them and Finland that, he believed, legitimised this policy action.

In April of 1990, President Koivisto gave an interview with a Finnish current affairs program to explain his actions.[2] Ingrians, he declared, were Finns, not Russians. They lived in Russia through accident of history, not desire, and were Lutheran like Finns, not Orthodox, like Russians. This, I argue, is an example of a Finnish politician creating a characteristic that he believes defines part of the Finnish identity, in this case being a Lutheran, and in turn using that to legitimise an act of connection, in this case an immigration policy. The idea was that Finns are traditionally Lutheran, and Ingrians are traditionally Lutheran, thus Ingrians should be considered Finns. This is problematic, as Finns have never been a completely Lutheran group. There is a long-established Finnish Orthodox Church, not to mention other religious minorities represented amongst Finnish citizens. Thus, the right to return for Ingrians, and the political discourses around it, actually presented several characteristics of Finnish identity that were limiting, problematicly and not, or no longer representative of the community of Finnish citizens.

Finnish Identity and the Right to Return Law

A reading of the political discussion on the Ingrian Finnish return migration gives five broad characteristics of Finnish identity that Finnish politicians saw as policy justification. They were the Lutheran religion, the Finnish language, an ancestral connection to the Finnish homeland, a feeling of being Western European and culturally connected to Scandinavia and the West, and a feeling of antagonism towards Russia, the constant threat to Finland's stability, or even existence. This was very much informed by collective memory of the Second World War. As a complete account of all constructions of Finnish identity used by Finnish lawmakers in this policy example would be beyond the scope of this paper, I have limited the analysis provided here to one significant case study: the Finnish language. Finnish national identity constructed around the Finnish language is a potentially surprising identity discourse, given that Finland is officially a bilingual country. Yet the Finnish language does appear to hold a particular significance for Finnish politicians in their constructions of Finnish identity. The historian Derek Fewster (2006) argues that the early Finnish nationalists who called for independence from Russia in the nineteenth century, including J.V. Snellman, believed Finland was a linguistic national community of Finnish speakers. According to this ideology, the Finnish language defines Finland as separate from its neighbours, and thus every Finnish speaker has a connection to Finland. When talking about Ingrians, some Finnish politicians in the late 1980s and early 1990 (before many Ingrians had actually arrived in Finland) argued along these lines, establishing Finnish language ability as something that proved Ingrians' Finnish connection. For instance, a group of Social Democrat MPs in 1989 requested that the Finnish government sponsor Finnish language classes for Ingrian children, and Finnish cultural events in Ingrian for adults, so that Ingrians could develop their 'own' language.[3] The 'own' language of Ingrians is Finnish, not Russian, which connects them to the Finnish government, though they are not Finnish citizens, as only the Finnish government can promote and maintain their linguistic identity.

However, there was further change to come for Finland that year, and further change to come for the Ingrian Finnish immigration program. The 1980s had been a period of economic expansion and falling unemployment in Finland, and by 1990, there was, in fact, an acute labour shortage in southern Finland, which was hampering further growth. Finnish politicians suggested Ingrian Finnish workers could help ameliorate this situation. And then, in the mid-90s, the situation changed dramatically. A severe economic recession hit, and unemployment began to rise. Suddenly, the return of Ingrian Finns seemed a more difficult project. There would be no jobs waiting for them when they arrived. Over the course of the rest of the 1990s and into the 2000s, the political discourse on the Ingrian return policy changed, and politicians became far less enthusiastic than they had been. Reforms in 1996 and 2002 introduced criteria that limited applicants, and finally in 2010, the policy was effectively ended. In particular, some of the same characteristics of Finnishness or Finnish identity that had proven the Finnishness of Ingrians, and were used to justify the appropriateness of the return policy, were now used to disprove the Finnishness of Ingrians, and the appropriateness of the policy. Using the same characteristic as before, the Finnish language, essentially the idea was thus: initially, Ingrians were Finnish because they did speak Finnish, and now, Ingrians are not Finnish because they do not speak Finnish, or do not speak Finnish well. For instance, in a 1998 statement to parliament from a group of National Coalition MPs, the government was warned that only a fifth of Ingrian returnees spoke Finnish, and that the policy had given Finland a monolingual Russian-speaking minority that was socially excluded and unemployed.[4] Whereas Finnish politicians in the 1980s and early 1990s had assumed that Ingrians could speak Finnish, now there was an experience of having Ingrians in Finland. Many Ingrians had grown up in wholly Russian-speaking communities, and spoke little or no Finnish (Hilson, 2008). Faced with this, Finnish politicians could have done one of two things: reassess the significance of the Finnish language as a characteristic of Finnishness, for here were Finns that spoke no Finnish, or alternatively, reassess the appropriateness of the return policy, for those who spoke no Finnish could not be taken to be Finns. By rolling back, and ultimately ending the return policy, Finnish politicians, for the most part, chose the latter option. This appears indicative of how strong the notion of Finnishness is in Finnish politics. One can take the experience of the Ingrian Finnish policy as an instance in which Finnish political discourse constructed national identity quite consistently, defining the Finnish community by language, even when it meant reassessing, so to speak, the Finnishness of a specific community.

Nicholas Prindiville

Ideology vs. Reality? Demographics in Finland

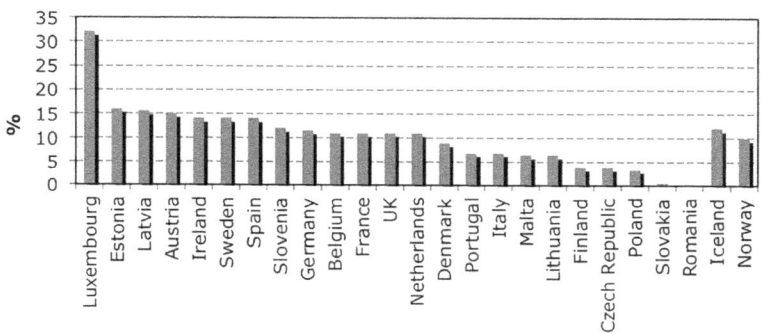

Figure 1

Foreign-born population as percentage of total population in European nations, 31 December 2008. Finland is at less than 5%, ranking 19th out of the 23 states included in the survey. Based on data from the Eurostat statistical book Migrants in Europe: A Statistical Portrait of the First and Second Generation, Brussels: European Union, 2011.

Figure 1 shows the relative size of immigrant communities in EU nations, plus Norway and Iceland, in 2008. The relative number of migrants living in Finland is much smaller than in any other West European nations - Finland has one of Western Europe's most limited migrant communities, and more homogenous populations. If, other than the new Ingrian return migrants, there were no significant communities living in the Finnish national community that did not conform to the characteristics of Finnishness promoted by Finnish politicians here, there would perhaps be no significant ideological inconsistency in questioning Ingrian conformity to the vision of Finnishness shaped by these characteristics.

COUNTRY	1990	1995	1996	1997	1998	1999	2000
Estonia	N/A	8,446	9,038	9,689	10,340	10,652	10,839
Former USSR	4,181	6,163	5,187	4,675	3,628	2,966	2,447
Former Yugoslavia	75	2,407	2,527	2,541	2,518	2,521	2,371
Russian Federation	N/A	9,720	11,810	14,316	16,861	18,575	20,552
Somalia	44	4,044	4,555	5,238	5,371	4,410	4,190
United States	1,475	1,844	1,833	1,905	2,001	2,063	2,010
Iraq	107	1,341	1,855	2,435	2,670	2,960	3,102
Vietnam	292	2,084	2,143	2,171	1,965	1,840	1814

Figure 2

Persons of select most-common non-EU nationalities resident in Finland, 1990 and 1995-2000. Based on data from Statistics Finland database Nationality According to Age and Sex by Region, 1990-2011.

However, *Figure 2* shows the figures for the number of migrants from select non-EU nationalities living in Finland in 1990, and from 1995 to 2000. The numbers are small, but one sees that in every instance, they increased. Finland is becoming an increasingly diverse nation, and one may not assume that new migrants to Finland conform to the identity characteristics Finnish politicians were endorsing when introducing the Ingrian Finnish return policy. For instance, many of the Somali immigrants who arrived in the 1990s were not Lutheran, but rather Muslim. Should their Finnish-born descendants be excluded from feeling Finnish because they have no connection to the Finnish Lutheran Church? This inconsistency between reality and ideology in the political discourse around the Ingrian return policy shows what Wodak et al. term 'the dogmatic, essentialist and naturalizing conceptions of nation and national identity' that prevent 'equal pluralistic co-existence of various ethnic groups, language communities, religious communities and forms of life' (1999: 9). The form of identity promoted by lawmakers in the Ingrian Right to Return policy, either in defence or repudiation of Ingrians' Finnishness, discriminates against other groups who already live in Finland, and prevents equal recognition of the variety of Finnish citizens whose connection to the country fails to comply to its effectively ethnic-essentialist parameters.

Notes

[1] 'Address by Mr Pertti Paasio, Minister for Foreign Affairs of Finland, at the Dinner on the Occasion of the 70th Anniversary of Finnish-United States Diplomatic Relations, Washington DC, November 8, 1989', in P. Paasio and M. Koivisto, *Finland in the Changing Europe: Major Speeches by Dr Mauno Koivisto, President of Finland, and Mr. Pertti Paasio, Minister for Foreign Affairs*, Helsinki: Ulkoasiainministeriön Julkaisuja, 1990.

[2] The interview was conducted by Ilkka Saari and Eero Ojanpera for *Ajankohtainen kakkonen*, a current affairs program on Finnish television station YLE TV2, and broadcast on 10 April 1990.

[3] The initiative was sponsored by Social Democrats Jouni Backman, Timo Roos, Marja-Liisa Tykkyläinen, Jukka Gustafsson and Kari Urpilainen, 'Määrärahan osoittamisesta inkerinsuomalaisten nuorten koulutusohjelmia varten', RA 1301/1989, in the Finnish Parliamentary Records book *Valtiopäivät 1989: Asiakirjat E4*, Helsinki: Eduskunta, 1989, p. 1363.

[4] Ilkka Kanerva, Ben Zyskowicz and Suvi Lindén, 'Inkeriläisten maahanmuuttoedellytyksistä', KVN 43/1998, available online at URL: <http://217.71.145.20/TRIPviewer/show.asp?tunniste=KVN+43/1998&base=erkys&palvelin=www.eduskunta.fi&f=WP>, accessed 4 November 2012.

Works Cited

Backman, Juoni, Roos, Timo, Tykkyläinen, Marja-Liisa, Gustafsson, Jukka and Urpilainen, Kari. 'Määrärahan osoittamisesta inkerinsuomalaisten nuorten koulutusohjelmia varten.', RA 1301/1989. *Valtiopäivät 1989: Asiakirjat E4*, Helsinki: Eduskunta, 1989, 1363.

Eurostat. *Migrants in Europe: A Statistical Portrait of the First and Second Generation, statistical book.* Brussels: European Union, 2011.

Fewster, Derek. *Visions of Past Glory: Nationalism and the Construction of Early Finnish History.* Helsinki: Finnish Literature Society, 2006.

Harinen, Päivi, Pitkänen, Pirkko, Sagne, Silvain and Jussi Ronkainen. 'Multiple Citizenship as a Challenge for Finnish Citizenship Policy Today.' Kalekin-Fishman, D. and Pitkänen, P., Eds, *Multiple Citizenship as a Challenge to European Nation-States*, Rotterdam: Sense, 2007, 121-44.

Hilson, Mary. *The Nordic Model: Scandinavia since 1945.* London: Reaktion Books, 2008.

Hjelm, Titus. 'Discourse Analysis', in Stausberg, M. and Engler, S., Eds, *The Routledge Handbook of Methods in the Study of Religion.* London and New York: Routledge, 2011, 134-50.

Kanerva, Ilkka, Zyskowicz, Ben and Suvi Lindén. 'Inkeriläisten maahanmuuttoedellyksistä, *KVN* 43/1998.' 4 November 2012 <http://217.71.145.20/TRIPviewer/show.asp?tunniste=KVN+43/1998&base=erkys&palvelin=www.eduskunta.fi&f=WP>

Kirwan, Frank and Frank Harrigan. 'Swedish-Finnish Return Migration, Extent Timing and Information Flows.' *Demography.* Vol. 23. No. 3, 1986, 313-27.

Koivisto, Mauno. 'Interview – Mauno Koivisto.' *Ajankohtainen kakkonen*, YLE TV2, 10 April 1990.

Maahanmuuttovirasto. 'Returnees.' 17 August 2010. <http://www.migri.fi/netcomm/content.asp?path=8,2475>

Maahanmuuttovirasto. 'Persons Coming from the Former Soviet Union.' 17 August 2010 <http://www.migri.fi/netcomm/content.asp?path=8,2475,2525>

Malinen, Pirkko. 'The Ingrian-Finnish Remigrants: Factors Preventing and Promoting Integration.' Teinonen, M. and T. J. Virtanen, Eds. *Ingrians and Neighbours: Focus on the Eastern Baltic Sea Region.* Helsinki: Finnish Literature Society, 1999, 195-210.

Mead, W. R. 'Finland in a Changing Europe.' *The Geographical Journal*, Vol. 157, No. 3, 1991, 307-15.

Nylund-Oja, Marja, Pentikäinen, Juha, Horn, Frank, Jaakola, Magdalena and Laura Yli-Vakkuri. 'Finnish Emigration and Immigration.' Pentikäinen, J. and M. Hiltunen, Eds. *Cultural Minorities in Finland: An Overview towards Cultural Policy.* Helsinki: Finnish National Commission for UNESCO, 1995, 173-223.

Paasi, Anssi. *Territories, Boundaries and Consciousness: The Changing Geographies of the Finnish-Russian Border.* Chichester: John Wiley and Sons, 1996.

Paasio, Pertti. 'Address by Mr Pertti Paasio, Minister for Foreign Affairs of Finland, at the Dinner on the Occasion of the 70th Anniversary of Finnish-United States Diplomatic Relations, Washington DC, November 8, 1989.' Paasio, P. and M. Koivisto. *Finland in the Changing Europe: Major Speeches by Dr Mauno Koivisto, President of Finland, and Mr. Pertti Paasio, Minister for Foreign Affairs*, Helsinki: Ulkoasiainministeriön Julkaisuja, 1990.

Paasio, Pertti and Mauno Koivisto. *Finland in the Changing Europe: Major Speeches by Dr Mauno Koivisto, President of Finland, and Mr. Pertti Paasio, Minister for Foreign Affairs.* Helsinki: Ulkooslainministeriön Julkaisuja, 1990.

Rimpiläinen, Sanna. 'Ingrian Finnishness as a Historical Construction.' The Organization Board of the Coimbra Group Working Party for Folklore and Ethnology, Ed. *Migration, Minorities, Compensation: Issues of Cultural Identity in Europe*, Brussels: Coimbra Group, 2001, 101-10.

Statistics Finland. *Nationality According to Age and Sex by Region, 1990-2011*, online statistics database. 21 September 2012 <http://pxweb2.stat.fi/Dialog/varval.asp?ma=020_vaerak_tau_101_en&ti=Nationality+according+to+age+and+sex+by+region+1990+-+2011&path=../Database/StatFin/vrm/vaerak/&lang=1&multilang=en>

Wodak, Ruth, de Cillia, Rudolf, Reisigl, Martin and Karin Liebhart. *The Discursive Construction of National Identity*. Trans. Angelika Hirsch and Richard Mitten. Edinburgh: Edinburgh University Press, 1999.

Granting Grið, Mercy and Peace: The Treatment of Opponents in War in Eleventh to Thirteenth Century Norway and Denmark

Louisa Taylor
University College London

In the early 1990s, John Gillingham noted that whilst there had been much discussion about 'codes of chivalry' and the attitudes and conventions which were followed by military elites in the medieval period, there had been little attention on how those rules and norms actually worked to limit brutality against the defeated in battle. Few have asked questions such as 'when did warfare become less harsh?' and 'for whom?' (Gillingham, 2000: 51). In recent times, historians like Matthew Strickland, in *War and Chivalry* (1996), and Richard Kaeuper, in *Chivalry and Violence in Medieval Europe* (1999), have looked at these questions in relation to Western Europe; however, the Scandinavian region is often left out of these discussions. Scandinavia is often seen as not developing the kinds of ideals of behaviour which we see from the eleventh century in England which, for example, encourage elite men to capture and ransom, rather than kill, their elite opponents in warfare. This article will argue that Norwegian and Danish narrative histories suggest that it was considered ideal for elites in these countries to restrain their violent behaviour once warfare had ceased. There was an ideal that these men should act mercifully towards those they had defeated in battle and respect those who had similar cultural beliefs and ideals to them.

It should be noted that this article discusses ideal behaviours, social norms, and expected behaviours; not necessarily what happened in practice. Whilst what happened in practice is important, limitations of space mean this will not be considered here. In this article, ideals of behaviour will be examined beyond the sometimes narrow search for the perfect rules of 'chivalry' or 'courtliness'. Indeed, we miss much if we do not broaden the questions we are asking. Matthew Strickland has argued that lords and their men shared common customs of warfare and ideas of appropriate behaviour perhaps as far back as the ninth century. This common 'martial culture' changed across the twelfth century but was not a new innovation (Strickland, 1996: 22). Therefore, it does not make sense to be looking for a strict set of rules to govern behaviour. Instead, David Crouch's use of Pierre Bourdieu's idea of 'habitus' gets us closer to the more fluid nature of human behaviour. According to Bourdieu, 'habitus' is 'the environment of behavioural and material expectations [...] which all societies and classes generate'. Importantly, the habitus is not codified; people learn to understand it through experiencing it (Crouch, 2005: 52-3). This article will therefore examine the learned expectations of behaviour as portrayed within Danish and Norwegian historical narratives.

The kings' sagas are the main narrative source for the medieval period before the second half of the thirteenth century in Norway. Composed in vernacular Old Norse, these take as their subject the history of Norwegian kings but were not necessarily produced in Norway. Whilst their authors were often Icelanders who lived in Norway, it has been suggested that *Fagrskinna* may have been composed by a Norwegian.[1] For Denmark, the main narrative source is the Latin *Gesta Danorum* of Saxo Grammaticus, composed at the end of the twelfth to beginning of the thirteenth century.

Of course, using historical narratives means viewing the past through the filter of many influences. Genre, production, and political affiliations, amongst other external influences, alter the way in which information is presented to the historian. In particular, many historians have commented on how medieval historians often crafted their historical figures for particular ends, both in Scandinavian sagas as well as Latin and vernacular texts from across the rest of Europe (Lönnroth, 1970).[2] In her survey of Anglo-Norman histories, Jean Blacker (1994) has argued that whilst historical truth was valued by medieval authors, and both Latin and vernacular narratives claim they aim to convey the truth as far as possible, accurate portrayals of historical figures are not shown to be valued in the same way. Instead, figures were described using collections of ideal behaviours, or non-ideal behaviours, depending on the authors' intentions. Blacker argues that these characterisations can help us understand the kinds of qualities a particular society valued at a particular point in time (ibid.). This article will examine the kinds of ideals which are presented as positive within the representations of historical figures presented within these historical narratives in order to examine how elite men were expected to behave towards defeated opponents. As space is limited, this article shall focus on only a few specific examples of how the treatment of the defeated is presented in texts describing Denmark and Norway in this period, although other examples can be found elsewhere within this corpus.

In these texts, we often see kings and other elite leaders of factions granting mercy, or what is called *grið* in Norwegian sources, once a battle is over. This is often translated as 'mercy' or 'quarter', but has wider implications than that in both Latin and vernacular texts. By accepting mercy from the victor, the defeated is agreeing to join the victor's men, in principle switching sides, although this was not often as binding at it appears. Accepting mercy therefore meant accepting submission to your opponent and there are many examples of elite men refusing to accept mercy because of this. It should also be noted that those who had committed crimes would often not be granted mercy if it was decided they needed to be punished. This includes being punished for slaying someone's kinsmen. This article will focus on pardons granted in the moments after a battle has ended, although mercy can be granted, or not granted, in other situations. For consistency, the term 'mercy' will be used to refer to this phenomenon, although with the intention of referring to the wider range of behaviour just described.

Turning to the kings' sagas, we can see how the granting of mercy is portrayed in texts taking Norway as their subject. Following one battle described in *Fagrskinna*, probably composed in the 1220s, King Haraldr Sigurðarson grants mercy to a man called Jarl Finnr Árnason, clearly a relatively important person given his title of jarl, which is similar to the position of an earl in England. The saga describes the episode:

> Þá svaraði konungrinn: "Villtu hafa grið, þó at þat sé ómakligt." Þá sagði jarlinn: "Eigi af hundinum þínum." "Villtu hafa grið af Magnúsi, frænda þínum?" Hann stýrði þá skipi. Jarlinn sagði: "Hvat mum hvelpr sá ráða griðum?" Þá hló konungrinn ok þótti gaman at eiga við hann ok mælti:, "Villtu taka grið af Þóru, frændkonu þinni?" [...] Þá mælti Finnr eitt orðskrǫk, þat er síðan er uppi haft, hversu reiðr hann var, er hann fekk eigi stillt orðum sínum: "Eigi er undarligt, at þú hafir vel bitizk í dag, er merrin hefir fylgt þér." Finni jarli váru gefin grið, ok var hann með Haraldi konungi um hríð. (Einarsson, 1985: 269)
>
> Then the King answered, "Will you accept quarter, although it is not deserved?"
> Then said the jarl, "Not from you, dog."

> "Will you accept quarter from your kinsman Magnús?" He was commanding a ship then.
> The Jarl said, "How can that whelp offer quarter?"
> Then the king laughed and found it fun to have to do with him, and said, "Will you accept quarter from your kinswoman Þóra?" [...]
> Then Finnr uttered a nasty speech that has since been remembered, showing how angry he was, so that he was unable to restrain his speech: "No wonder you have bitten hard today, since the mare has come with you."
> Jarl Finnr was given quarter, and he stayed with King Haraldr for a while. (Finlay, 2004: 214)

Another kings' saga, *Morkinskinna*, composed around 1220, also describes this incident and goes on to add:

> Ok í annan stað, er sagt var áðr frá orðaviðskiptum þeira Haralds konungs ok Finns jarls; þar líknaði sá er valdit átti, ok vegr var þat en eigi lítilræði. (Jakobsson and Ingi Guðjónsson, 2011: 253)

> Moreover, when the exchange of words between King Haraldr and Finnr jarl was told, the man who had the power showed mercy, and there was honour in that action and no lack of authority. (Andersson and Gade, 2000: 232)

Granting *grið*, or mercy, to a defeated elite opponent is shown to give a person honour through displaying the virtue of mercy. In theory, it does not diminish a leader's authority, but rather shows him to be practising the ideal behaviours of a virtuous warrior after a battle.

This episode is rather jovial in tone considering a man's life hangs in the balance. This joking tone regarding the norms of granting pardons suggests the author believes his audience to be fairly comfortable with ideal behaviour following battle and its conventions – comfortable enough to describe this process as a kind of negotiation. In many ways, negotiation is the best way to describe how episodes like these are portrayed in medieval narratives. Whilst granting mercy is presented as ideal behaviour for elite men in Denmark and Norway in this period, those who accept mercy are also accepting the submission and loss of honour that goes with it. This means that we often see, just as in this example, elite men refusing pardons and opting instead to fight on in honour or be killed.

Turning to Denmark and the *Gesta Danorum* of Saxo Grammaticus, we see that even in wars against other kingdoms there is an ideal that mercy should be granted to defeated opponents. It should be noted that there are many examples of heathens being slaughtered for refusing to convert to Christianity throughout medieval history. Crusading movements dominated much of the medieval period. Indeed, elsewhere in the *Gesta*, Saxo even muses, 'what kind of sacrifice could we consider more pleasing to the Almighty than the slaughter of wicked men?'[3] However, it is interesting to see that mercy is still promoted by historical narratives even in some of these situations and especially for those who choose to convert.

Much of the Gesta Danorum deals with the Danish invasions of the Baltic and their attempts to conquer and Christianise the people of that region. Even in the wars against the Slavs we see Saxo Grammaticus, the author of this text, suggesting it was more worthy for a person to be merciful rather than ruthless to defeated opponents. This episode recounts the story of the Danish army attacking a Slavic fortress. The Danes quickly overcome their Slavic enemy and the leaders of the region come to ask for a truce. The Slavs promise to pay compensation to the Danes and also return Danish prisoners they were holding. Archbishop Absalon, the right hand man of the twelfth century King Valdemar I, is shown considering this request as one of the king's advisors. Absalon suggests that:

> [...] quarum usus perniciosus patrie sed gratus, contemptus uero commodior quam charior esset futurus. (Friis-Jensen and Zeeberg, 2005: 478)

> [...] to accept them would be welcome to our country, but injurious to its interest, while to reject them would be more advantageous, but not so acceptable. (Christiansen, 1981: 578)

Absalon, as he is portrayed here, seems aware that it is not so 'acceptable' to refuse an offer of surrender even if would be more profitable to carry on the war. Peace is ultimately the more acceptable, and apparently 'welcome', option. The episode continues:

> Siquidem pecuniam regi, pacem ciuibus, captiuis missionem pacti nomine lucrari fauori quam utilitati propius emolumentum esse, iisdem uero pro nihilo ductis a bello non recedere saluberimum. (Friis-Jensen and Zeeberg, 2005: 478)

> For they would get more popularity than practical advantage if they obtained money for the king, peace for the people and the return of the captives; it would be most profitable of all to carry on fighting, and get these things for nothing. (Christiansen, 1981: 578)

The Danes opt to go for the most popular action: to sue for peace (Christiansen, 1981: 578). Saxo is suggesting that it is more acceptable, more praiseworthy, to grant mercy to those who have asked for it, even at the expense of profit.

There are religious elements running through both Danish and Norwegian portrayals of the granting of mercy. Examples of kings being merciful to those they have defeated echo the well-known medieval trope of the 'forgiving king'.[4] We see this particularly clearly in the *Sverris Saga*, the saga of King Sverrir of Norway composed across the late twelfth and early thirteenth century. Sverrir became king of all Norway after defeating his opponent for the throne, and sometimes co-ruler, King Magnús, and his band of men, the Croziers. His victory came after an extended period of civil war, during which both sides committed many devastating attacks on the opposing side. During this conflict, Sverrir's men besiege the rock of Tunsberg, a rocky island out to sea, occupied by Sverrir's enemies, the Croziers. After a time some of the Croziers leave the rock and ask for mercy from Sverrir, which he grants to them. After hearing that Sverrir was willing to grant mercy to his enemies, the leader of the Croziers stationed on the rock asks for mercy for the whole of his force in return for their surrender. Sverrir asks his men if they would agree to such an offer. Understandably, Sverrir's men are reluctant to grant mercy to this enemy force given that, as per the rules of granting mercy, any pardoned men would become part of Sverrir's force. They are concerned that they would be forced to share their cabins with their former tormentors. However, Sverrir explains to them that by forgiving others they will earn forgiveness from God for their sins (Hauksson, 2007: 267-278):

> Hér í Túnsbergi felldu Baglar Híða, bróður minn, en í Osló Philippum jarl, frænda minn ok marga aðra, en nú í vetr munu þér heyrt hafa at þeir hafa Sverri kallat bikkju eðr meri ok mǫrgum ǫðrum illum nǫfnum. Nú vil ek þat fyrirgefa þeim fyrir Guðs sakir ok vænta þar á mót af honum fyrirgefningar

þess er ek hefi honum á móti gǫrt. Eigu þér ekki síðr sálur en ek ok eigið þess at minnask. Engi maðr mun kalla yðr at heldr bleyðimenn fyrir þessa sǫk. (Hauksson, 2007: 277)

Here in Tunsberg the Bagals [Croziers] slew Hidi, my brother; and in Oslo, Earl Philippus, my kinsman, and many besides. And now this winter you must have heard them call Sverri dog, mare, and many other bad names. I am willing to forgive them for God's sake, and I hope from Him, in return, forgiveness of all I have done against Him. You have souls no less than I, and must bear this in mind. No man will ever call you cowards any the more because you so act. (Sephton, 1899: 229-230)

Again we are told that forgiveness and granting mercy to opponents is not the act of a coward, but one of a man who has one eye on his immortal soul. This passage is placed just before King Sverrir's death scene, providing an excuse for the author to amplify the virtues of his protagonist.

Yet there is another more secular reason which seems involved in some decisions to grant mercy presented in these narratives. One reason why elite men in particular are seen as wanting to avoid killing other elite men in post-conquest England is out of respect for a shared code of behaviour, or shared values of warfare (Gillingham, 2000; Strickland, 2001). We see a similar admiration in Norway and Denmark which sometimes encourages a more merciful attitude towards some defeated opponents, although not all. This can even extend to those who are technically 'outside' of elite society.

Saxo Grammaticus presents this idea in the *Gesta Danorum*. During one sea patrol a group of Danes led by two men named Esbernus and Wethemannus come across a group of pirate ships and engage in battle with them. One pirate, Mirocus, performs 'acts of gallantry' during the battle, leaping onto the Danes' ship alone to continue the battle (Christiansen, 1981: 546). Even though he is captured the Danes agree to let him go free in respect of his bravery:

> Cuius respectui tantum uenerationis a uictoribus tributum est, ut, quum captus supplicium mereretur, redemptionem acceperit, potiusque in eo probitas honorata sit quam facinora punita. Ita quum impietati pernicies deberetur, fortitudini salus donata est. (Friis-Jensen and Zeeberg, 2005: 432)

> He [Mirocus] was so respected by the conquerors that after he had been captured and was due for punishment, he got his release, and was honoured for his constancy, rather than punished for his crimes. Thus although he deserved death for his wickedness, he was granted his life for his bravery. (Christiansen, 1981: 546)

Esbernus and Wethemannus are probably elite men, given that they own the four long-ships being used to patrol for pirates and are also named within the text. This episode shows two Danish elite men identifying their own ideals in their opponents, especially prowess, bravery, and not running away from a battle, and granting them a pardon out of respect for these.

Even though mercy could be granted to a wide range of people, the actual act of granting mercy is shown within historical narratives to be dependent on the opinion of the most powerful man present. The issue for the historian, however, is that these powerful men are often the main protagonists within our extant source material. Therefore, one may struggle to gain a complete picture of how merciful behaviour was being used. Could a person who was not the leader of a faction, a king, a pretender to the throne or a powerful magnate, take the decision to act mercifully towards defeated opponents? In our texts the granting of mercy is often shown to be the preserve of the elite, and these texts seem to suggest that whilst those lower in status could grant mercy, they could equally be overruled by their lord.

An example from *Sverris Saga* shows that whilst those of a lower status could grant mercy, their lord had the final decision. In a speech before a battle, the author of *Sverris Saga*, Karl Jonsson, has King Sverrir tell his men to remember how their opponents, the Croziers, have treated them in the past, exhorting them to 'give quarter to no man, except those who come before me' (Sephton, 1899: 201). Yet some in his force, called the Birkibeins, do give quarter to their kinsmen during the battle. The fact that this happens and also that the author of the saga shows Sverrir as needing to warn his men against giving quarter to their kinsmen, suggests the author at least thought this kind of behaviour was possible at that time. The saga continues thus:

> En er liðit kom í bœinn upp þá reyndisk þat at sveitarhǫfðingjar hǫfðu gefit grið Bǫglum, frændum sínum ok vinum. En sumir Birkibeinar minntusk hvat konungr hafði um rœtt. Var þar at gengit í stofu nǫkkurri þar er Baglar váru inni, ok váru þeir drepnir. En þeira frændr, er grið hǫfðu gefit þeim, gengu þá til konungs ok kærðu fyrir honum. Konungr kvaðsk sjá til gott ráð, at þeir leitaði at þessum mǫnnum er drepit hǫfðu frændr þeira ok bað þá þar hefna. Eftir þat gengu sveitirnar um bœinn, ok hendu þá hvárir annarra frændr þar til er allir váru drepnir. (Hauksson, 2007: 245)

> When the force came into the town, it was found that many captains of companies had given quarter to Bagals [Croziers] who were their kinsmen and friends. Some of the Birkibeins, remembering the King's charge, went into a sitting-room

> containing Bagals [Croziers] and slew them; and the kinsmen who had given these men quarter went before the King and complained to him. The King answered that he saw a good remedy; let them find out if those who had slain their kinsmen had given quarter to any kinsmen of their own, and he bade them avenge themselves. After this, parties went through the town, each picking out the other's kinsmen until all the Bagals [Croziers] were slain. (Sephton, 1899: 202-3)

The author of Sverris Saga, Karl Jonsson, presents elite men as in theory in charge of granting mercy as an extension of their role as leader of a military force.

Historical narratives from Norway and Denmark show the ideal of granting mercy to the defeated after battle as something elite men should practice firstly as a result of their Christian faith and secondly out of respect for their fellow elite men. The elite male group in these countries shared a set of military values and a set of expected behaviours. Not killing those they had defeated who shared those values and ideals is presented as a common ideal by the authors of contemporary histories. These medieval texts show there were potentially systems of restraining violence from the twelfth century onwards. The problem is, of course, deciding to what extent these texts reflect reality. Are they reflecting a common religious culture amongst their authors, who had been mostly educated by the Church, rather than the mentality of warriors at this time? As these texts show reasons for granting mercy beyond just following the teachings of the Christian Church, in this case a respect for shared military values and ideals, it is possible to suggest that these texts are reflecting some of those societies' discourses around violence and mercy. The different discourses of mercy are prevalent across most of Europe at this time, in a range of texts, also suggests that the promotion of ideals of mercy was a real concern at this time across a wide geographical area. Sources for Norway and Denmark portray the granting of mercy as a positive behaviour in a similar way to historical narratives from England and western-Europe in the eleventh to thirteenth centuries. This suggests that the kind of behaviours presented as ideal for warriors in Scandinavia were not always far away from those we see in the narratives of western-Europe.

Notes

[1] Cases for both Icelandic and Norwegian authorship of Fagrskinna have been put forward. For more on this discussion, see Alison Finlay's introduction to her translation of the text. (Finlay, 2004: 14-17)

[2] In 1970 Lars Lönnroth discussed how scholars at that time mostly saw the Icelandic family sagas as 'objective' narratives, which contained very little moral reasoning or evidence of rhetorical crafting. Lönnroth argues, however, that these texts are subject to the same rhetorical crafting as other European texts, especially in terms of their crafting of historical figures to be seen as positive or negative characters. (cf. Lönnroth, 1970; Lönnroth, 1969; Harris, 1986)

[3] Quod enim sacrificii genus scelestorum nece diuinę potentię iocundius existimemus? (Friis-Jensen and Zeeberg, 2005: 524)

[4] Hans Jacob Orning (2008) discusses the presentation of the king as a 'forgiving lord' according to the Christian ideal, arguing that this is a general feature of kingship and not something which is personally attributed to individual kings.

Works Cited

Blacker, Jean. *The Faces of Time: Portrayal of the Past in Old French and Latin Historical Narrative of the Anglo-Norman Regnum*. Austin: University of Texas Press, 1994.

Crouch, David. *The Birth of Nobility: Constructing Aristocracy in England and France 900-1300*. Harlow: Pearson, 2005.

Danorum Regum Heroumque Historia: Books X-XVI. 3 vols. Ed. and trans. Eric Christiansen. Vol. II. Oxford: B.A.R., 1981.

Fagrskinna A Catalogue of the Kings of Norway, A Translation with Introduction and Notes. Ed. and trans. Alison Finlay. Leiden: Brill, 2004.

Fagrskinna: Nóregs konunga tal' in Ágrip af Nóregs konunga Sǫgum. Fagrskinna - Nóregs konunga tal. Ed. Bjarni Einarsson. Íslenzk fornrit XXIX. Reykjavík: Hið íslenzka fornritafélag, 1985.

Gillingham, John. 'Conquering the Barbarians: War and Chivalry in Twelfth-Century Britain.' *The English in the Twelfth Century: Imperialism, National Identity, and Political Values*. Ed. Idem. Woodbridge: The Boydell Press, 2000. 41-58 (first publ. in The Haskins Society Journal 4 (1992): 67-84).

Harris, Joseph. 'Saga as Historical Novel.' Structure and Meaning in Old Norse Literature: *New Approaches to Textual Analysis and Literary Criticism*. Eds John Lindow, Lars Lönnroth and Gerd Wolfgang Weber. Odense: Odense University Press, 1986, 87-219.

Kaeuper, Richard W. *Chivalry and Violence in Medieval Europe*. Oxford: Oxford University Press, 1999.

Lönnroth, Lars. 'Rhetorical Persuasion in the Sagas.' *Scandinavian Studies* 42.2, 1970, 157-189.

---. 'The Noble Heathen: A Theme in the Sagas.' *Scandinavian Studies* 41, 1969, 1-29.

Morkinskinna I. Eds. Ármann Jakobsson and Þórður Ingi Guðjónsson. Íslenzk fornrit XXIII. Reykjavík: Hið íslenzka fornritafélag, 2011.

Morkinskinna: The Earliest Icelandic Chronicle of the Norwegian Kings (1030-1157). Ed. and trans. Theodore M. Andersson and Kari Ellen Gade. Ithaca: Islandica Li, 2000.

Orning, Hans Jacob. *Unpredictability and Presence: Norwegian Kingship in the High Middle Ages*. Trans. Alan Crozier. Leiden: Brill, 2008.

Saxo Grammaticus Gesta Danorum Denmarkshistorien. 2 Vols. Latin text. Ed. Karsten Friis-Jensen. Trans. Peter Zeeberg. Vol. 1. København: Det Danske Sprog- og Litteraturselskab & Gads Forlag, 2005.

Strickland, Matthew J. War and Chivalry: *The Conduct and Perception of War in England and Normandy, 1066-1217*. Cambridge: Cambridge University Press, 1996.

---. 'Killing or Clemency? Ransom, Chivalry and Changing Attitudes to Defeated Opponents in Britain and Northern France, 7-12th centuries.' *Krieg im Mittelalter*. Ed. Hans-Henning Kortüm. Berlin: Akademie Verlag, 2001, 93-122.

Sverrissaga: The Saga of King Sverri of Norway. Ed. and trans. J. Sephton. London: David Nutt, 1899.

Sverris Saga. Ed. Þorleifur Hauksson. Íslenzk fornrit XXX. Reykjavík: Hið íslenzka fornritafélag, 2007.

Visibility, Authority, and Execution in Heimskringla

Keith Ruiter
University of York

Recent archaeological interest in assembly sites has yielded an impressive array of newly nuanced information about the relationship between authority and visibility in the physical, judicial, and social landscapes of medieval Scandinavia (Sanmark and Semple, 2008; Sanmark, 2009; Myrberg, 2008).[1] Though important on their own, the developments in archaeology call for similar progress to be attempted in related disciplines, in the hope of synthesising a more detailed picture.[2] This paper takes a preliminary step in this direction by considering the early sagas of *Heimskringla* with the relationship between authority and visibility in mind (Sturluson, 1964). By focussing on one particular expression of authority in these sagas – that of state-sanctioned judicial execution – this paper will attempt to trace how the evolution of Scandinavian power-structures is portrayed in *Heimskringla*.[3]

Heimskringla makes an excellent starting point for these considerations for a number of reasons. First, its largely uncontroversial attribution to Snorri Sturluson means that we have a comparatively good understanding of the literary and historical environment of which it is a product (Hollander, 1964: ix-xxvi). Second, its tendency to straddle the line between 'work of literature' and 'historical document' encourages a more interdisciplinary approach (ibid. xxi).[4] Third, and most importantly in this context, its sweeping chronology is very helpful for identifying and charting broad patterns and progressions (ibid. xvi-xvii). With this in mind, the paper will move forward on the following premises: that by consulting the broad sweep of *Heimskringla*'s chronology we might be able to track how authority was thought to have changed through the Viking Age, and furthermore that, by focussing on legal authority in general, and judicial execution in particular, we might be able to trace one microcosmic aspect of authority in the process of those changes.

With the scope of the paper laid out, we should spend a moment defining the idea of judicial execution as it pertains to our considerations here. Judicial execution occupies a unique space in early-medieval Scandinavian society in that it differs from practices like murder, human sacrifice, or death in or after battle in terms of intentionality. Rather, judicial execution is to be seen here as a judicially imperative killing, enacted on a convicted offender as a form of punishment in extreme cases of criminal deviance. In this way, it differs from murder in its operation within a legal framework; from human sacrifice in its legal, rather than cultic interests; and from death in or after battle in its attempted impartiality. Defined in this way, judicial execution stands out in the pages of *Heimskringla*.

Considering the Texts

Heimskringla opens with *Ynglinga Saga*, which traces the euhemerised semi-legendary origin of the line of kings (Sturluson, 1964: 6-50). The kings described often rule little more than a single locality and their legal authority is almost non-existent. Instead the saga paints the picture of a society used to forceful and bloody shows of military might and hall-burning as means to gain dominion. This is of course to be expected, as one must first have dominions in order to exercise legal authority, or any other type for that matter, over them. Despite this, it should be acknowledged that there is a rough proto-legal framework of cause and effect that arises from the various vignettes of the saga. This takes the form of a punishment of sorts, typically lethal in nature, following an action deemed to be worth avenging. Examples include King Dagr harrying at Vörva after a farmer kills his magic sparrow (ibid. 21); Skjálf hanging King Agni to avenge her father (ibid. 22-3); and King Gýlaugr hanging Jörundr to avenge his father (ibid. 27).

While a proto-legal framework of cause and effect can be seen in *Ynglingasaga*, in *Hálfdanar Saga Svarta*, we begin to see a more familiar legal authority emerging (Sturluson, 1964: 51-58). We are told that the king appointed officers to ensure justice was upheld in his realm (ibid. 53):

> Þá kom til hans Atli jarl inn mjóvi af Gaulum. Hann var vinr Hálfdanar konungs. Setti konungr han yfir Sygnafylki at dœma þar landslög ok heimta skatta til handa konungi. (Aðalbjarnarson, 1979: 86)

> Then he was joined by Earl Atli the Slender of Gaular. He was a friend of King Hálfdan, and the king set him over the Sogn district to speak judgement according to the laws of the land and to collect the taxes for the king. (Sturluson, 1964: 53)

We learn that the king himself was a just man, who set up penalties according to birth and merit in order to keep the peace:

> Hálfdan konungr var vizkumaðr mikill ok sannenda ok jafnaðar ok setti lög ok gætti sjálfr ok þrýsti öllum til at gæta, ok at eigi mætti ofsi steypa lögunum, gerði hann sjálfr saktal, ok skipaði hann bótum hverjum eptir sínum burð ok metorðum. (Aðalbjarnarson, 1979: 91)

> King Hálfdan was a very wise man, both truthful and fair-dealing. He both made laws and kept them himself. He compelled all to keep them; and in order that violence should not overthrow the laws, he set up penalties, fixing everyone's compensation according to his birth and position. (Sturluson, 1964: 57)

It is clear, however, that this legal system is far removed from one we might recognise today, or even Snorri himself might have recognised, as immediately after this last excerpt we are told how the king tortured a magically-inclined Finn to discover what became of his vanished banquet (ibid.).

We are told in *Haralds Saga Ins Hárfagra* that the eponymous king used law and tax paired with military might to help increase his dominions (Sturluson, 1964: 59-95). We also learn that this law was not strictly to garner support or secure his position, but also to maintain order, though this can seem secondary to his personal interests at times. It is further explained that Harald introduced a novel system of administration that was protected by his new laws (ibid. 63).[5]

Hákon the Good, the son of Harald Fairhair and foster-son of Æthelstan of England seemingly takes this legal progression further in his eponymous saga, instituting new taxes and changing the system of governance to suit his design (Sturluson, 1964: 96-127). According to Snorri the Gulathing and Frostathing laws, two of the oldest surviving law codes we have from medieval Norway (Larson, 1935), were laid down by Hákon (Sturluson, 1964: 104):

> Hann setti Gulaþingslög með ráði Þorleifs spaka, ok hann setti Frostaþingslög með ráði Sigurðar jarls ok annarra Þrœnda, þeira er vitrastir váru. En Heiðsævislög hafði sett Hálfdan svarti, sem fyrr er ritat. (Aðalbjarnarson, 1979: 163)

> He devised the Gulathings Law with the help of Thorleif the Wise; and the Frostathings Law, with the advice of Earl Sigurth and other men from the Trondheim district who were accounted wisest. But the Heithsævis Law had been given by Hálfdan the Black, as mentioned before. (Sturluson, 1964: 104)

These may have been regional rather than national laws as are familiar to us today, but Snorri's emphasis on them seems to suggest that they were novel and merit-worthy.

Yet, here we run into one of the infamous methodological issues of using saga-evidence in these sorts of discussions: that, to put it bluntly, Snorri has been proven to be factually wrong at times. Modern scholarship has shown that Hákon was not responsible for the founding of the Gulathing and Frostathing laws; at least one of these was already set up before his reign (Larson, 1935; Bagge, 2010; Sturluson, 1964: 104). Despite this apparent inaccuracy, the argument for a clear progression in legal interest and authority presented in *Heimskringla* remains sound. First, from a literary point of view, *Heimskringla*, as we receive it, indeed marks this progression, making it noteworthy from the perspective of authorial interest. Second, from a historiographic point of view, Snorri's attribution of these laws to Hákon could be due to vested interest, or it could be simple error, suggesting that this progression may have actually happened earlier than even Snorri realised. Furthermore, though Hákon may not have been responsible for initially making these laws as described, he certainly seems to have made every effort to make them his own, with a number of provisions in the laws directly attributed to him (Larson, 1935). With historians largely in agreement that many of these provisions are likely do date to this period, we should not be so quick to throw the baby out with the bathwater (Bagge, 2010: 179).

Therefore, we are left with a very clear progression in the legal authority in the earliest sagas of *Heimskringla*, from the distant past to the mid-tenth century (961 CE). Though Snorri's account may differ at times with what modern scholarship has revealed,[7] the overall pattern that emerges here is one very much in line with our growing understandings of power dynamics and authority in Viking Age Scandinavia – namely a marked growth in the importance of centralisation of authority (Thurston, 2002; Sanmark, 2009; Sanmark and Semple, 2008). Yet even more can be said by turning, finally, to the Saga of Óláf Tryggvason.

Óláfs saga Tryggvasonar

Óláfs saga Tryggvasonar (Sturluson, 1964: 144-244) is of particular interest here because it is descriptive of the legal landscape before Óláfr's reign and of the one he himself institutes, particularly in the case of executions. For example, in regard to the former, we are told of the capture of the Jómsvíkings who are subdued and bound by Þorkell Leira's men, himself a follower of Earl Eiríkr. Þorkelll lines the Jómsvíkings up immediately after the battle and is set to decapitate the lot of them with a large axe; however, he is halted by Earl Eiríkr who offers a legal pardon to the captives (ibid. 181-4). This, despite being an example of a post-combat execution scenario, is noteworthy as it seems that no formalised legal authority is required to condemn the Jómsvikings to death, yet it is apparently necessary to pardon them.

By comparison, Óláfr's own punitive attitude seems to be presented by Snorri as something different from what had come before him. This certainly makes sense, as Óláfr was attempting to introduce ecclesiastical law.[6] We learn that the people at first view his attempts to do away with the old religion as 'lawless' and a legal defense is prepared to combat it (Sturluson, 1964; 196-7); however, Óláfr appears to embrace and respect the laws while seeking to update them to correlate with his missionary agenda. For example, we learn that, in Rogaland, Óláfr does not simply coerce freeholders to his point of view, but rather declares his case at an assembly for all to hear. He even gives the opportunity to those gathered to speak their case in opposition, though the saga takes a hagiographic turn here and this is foiled by divine intervention (ibid.). We also learn that Óláfr is very shrewd at using legal settlements to buy time to bring the outcome to his favour, often by way of military force (ibid. 204-8), but events like the marriage settlement between his sister Ástríðr and Erlingr Skjálgsson in return for the willing Christianisation of the men of Horthaland belies a certain legal cunning and sophistication in Óláfr's actions.

As Óláf secures his hold, we see new legal details coming out in the text. In the proclamation he makes before the assembly at Túnsberg (Sturluson, 1964: 201-2), he declares warlocks, sorcerers, and magical-practitioners outlaws, meaning they had forfeited the safety of the law and could be killed with impunity (Larson, 1935; Brink, 2008). Though, upon examining Óláfr's domestic policy it would appear that anyone who did not accept Christianity was also viewed as an outlaw in Óláfr's eyes, as can be seen in his very forceful conversions. Yet, despite Óláfr's reputation for such things, Snorri's version of the story suggests that judicial violence was not always the first method he employed. In the example of Sigurðr and Haukr, two heathen merchants who were asked to convert and refused, we are told that Óláfr sought to change their minds in a number of ways. Though threats of torture and death were issued, the men were only imprisoned and Óláfr attempted to change their minds through reason (Sturluson, 1964: 209-10).

However, Óláfr was clearly not always feeling so gracious, particularly in the case of practitioners of magic. We are told that convicted warlocks were both burned and drowned (Sturluson,

1964: 201-3), Eyvindr Kinnrifa's stomach was burst by a pot of live coals being put on it (ibid. 211), and, in a particularly inventive execution, Óláfr arranged for a serpent to eat its way out of a sorcerer named Rauðr (ibid. 214). Regardless of whether the executions depicted are rooted in historical events or are simply literary devices, these vignettes do strongly suggest that Óláfr was remembered in part for his tendency to actively execute people, something we do not see in any legal capacity in *Heimskringla* until this saga. This does not suggest that Óláfr should be seen as the first Scandinavian king to execute people, rather it would appear that those recording his history saw Óláfr's use of execution as differing from his predecessors. The type of executions he orders also seem to be different from what we have seen thus far in some very important ways.

Óláfr's executions are always witnessed by members of his own following and, due to their public settings, the people of the locality in which they occur as well. The executions also seem to be highly memorable to the local population, in that Snorri suggests that particular toponyms – like 'Skrattasker' [Sorcerers' Skerries] (Sturluson, 1964; 203) – preserve the memory of their occurrence. It should also be noted that these public executions are often conducted in places associated with power and authority like on the steps of the temple at Mærin (ibid. 207-8), at Ögvaldsnes on the Island of Körmt (ibid. 202-3), and the island of Niðarhólmr (ibid. 192-3), suggesting an attempt by Óláfr to bring these places under his own sway.

In fact, regarding Niðarhólmr, there is one execution depicted in the saga that is particularly remarkable to our considerations here (Sturluson, 1964: 188-93). Karkr, a thrall, flees with Earl Hákon as Óláfr gains power in Þándheimr; the two eventually hide in a pigsty when Óláf, in pursuit of Hákon, comes to the farm where they are hiding. Unable to find Hákon, Óláf makes a speech within earshot of the fugitives, promising wealth and honour to the man who kills Hákon. Karkr, allegedly due to his cowardly nature, soon cracks under the pressure of their furtive condition, kills Hákon and takes his head to Óláfr. Things do not go as Karkr may have expected. As a thrall who has just lethally betrayed his lord, a very serious crime, Karkr is not repaid with wealth or honour, but with decapitation. Interestingly, though this execution is not described as taking place in a public setting, the heads of both Karkr and Hákon are brought to the island of Niðarhólmr which we are told 'was at that time used for putting to death thieves and evildoers, and a gallows stood there' (ibid. 192) ('Sá hólmr var þá hafðr til þess at drepa þar þjófa ok illmenni, ok stóð þar gálgi' (Aðalbjarnarson, 1979: 298)). Furthermore we are told that Óláfr had the heads of Karkr and Hákon fastened to the gallows and a large company of farmers proceeded to stone them.

This episode has great potential to be studied from the point of view of apotropaic behaviours or from the perspective of localised traditions of dispensing judicial violence, but here we should look at it from the point of view of visibility and authority. Not only are we told that this is a specified execution site, it is obviously linked to legal and political authority as well, being situated in full view of one of the most populous and powerful regions of the day, sitting in the Þándheimsfjord at the mouth of the Nið river, known as Nidelva today. This is further remarkable because it was at Þándheimr, in full view of Niðarhólmr and the gallows thereon, that Óláfr was chosen as king over Norway less than a year later. For a highly visual society, this would have made a very impressive and imposing backdrop indeed (Sturluson, 1964: 193-4).

Discussion and Conclusions

Not only does *Heimskringla* present us with one historian's interpretation of the increasingly complex power dynamics of Viking Age Scandinavia, it also showcases a logical progression in the legal power and authority thought to have been wielded by successive Norwegian rulers. This progression is very much in line with the picture, emerging from modern archaeological scholarship, of the centralisation of power in Scandinavia at this time (Thurston, 2002; Sanmark, 2009; Sanmark and Semple, 2008). One aspect of this legal power and authority is the use of judicial executions. The highly visual executions ordered by Óláfr Tryggvason are presented as markedly different from those of rulers before him – leaving us with the intriguing suggestion that aspects of his legal and royal structures were seen as novel and noteworthy by subsequent historians.

Though scholars like Michael H. Gelting, examining Denmark, point to the 'archaic' nature of royal and social systems at the end of the Viking Age (Gelting, 2011), the evidence in *Heimskringla* would suggest this was not the case in contemporary Norway. To paraphrase and reappropriate a point made by Sverre Bagge when discussing state-formation in Norway: Norwegian society and administrative systems at this time were not rotting, archaic things just waiting to be modernised by the right person at the right moment (Bagge, 2010; 11-19). Rather, Norwegian systems of authority and power have evolved throughout time to suit particular needs and react to specific stimuli – the later Viking Age being no exception (ibid.). In fact, in response to such ideas of 'archaicness,' it is important to point out, as Bagge does, that the legal and power systems implemented by Óláfr Tryggvason seem to be intriguingly similar to those utilised later in the medieval period. Bagge further argues for the existence of legal and authoritative structures from a very early date with a notable tendency toward the centralisation of these structures in the tenth and eleventh centuries (ibid.). In light of these assertions by Bagge, the above evidence – of a progression of legal authority in the later Viking Age in general, and of structures for judicial executions in particular – may add a new point of inquiry in current scholarly debates, particularly when compared to the work of scholars like Orning and Gelting, which suggests that the centralisation of authority did not happen until later in the medieval period.

As scholarship on these issues develops, it is important to bear in mind that judicial executions and the frameworks for their usage in society can be important indicators of the legal environment of their time. The dramatic, and highly memorable executions ordered by Óláfr certainly seem to be judicially grounded, and made public in ways previous executions presented in *Heimskringla* were not. They are conducted in places associated with past royal power, and in the case of Niðarhólmr, at the very doorstep of Óláfr's future power-base of Niðaros. Therefore, these executions should be viewed as another important, highly visible display of authority in a culture, which, as modern scholarship continues to suggest (Thurston 2002; Sanmark, 2009; Bagge, 2010), required such shows of force as they continued their evolution toward modern nationhood.

Notes

[1] For further information on the changing power dynamics during the Viking Age, see Thurston (2002).

[2] See Orning (2007) for an example of a recent work that attempts to make progress on this issue. Furthermore, see Moreland (2003) for a discussion of the importance and benefits of comparing archaeological and textual evidence and findings.

[3] For an introduction to the Viking Age and particulars of Scandinavia at this time see Richards (2005).

[4] For more on the peculiarities of *Heimskringla* see Bagge (1991); for the use of rhetorical devices in the sagas see Lönnroth (1970); and for more on the generic complexity of the sagas see Harris (1986).

[5] 'Haraldr konungr setti þann rétt allt þar, er hann vann ríki undir sik, at hann eignaðisk óðöl öll ok lét alla bóendr gjalda sér landskyldir, bæði ríka ok óríka. Hann setti jarl í hverju fylki, þann er dœma skyldi lög ok landsrétt ok heimta sakeyri ok landskyldir, ok skyldi jarl hafa þriðjung skatta ok skylda til borðs sér ok kostnaðar. Jarl hverr skyldi hafa undir sér fjóra hersa eða fleiri, ok skyldi hverr þeirra hafa tuttugu marka veizlu. Jarl hverr skyldi fá konungi í her sex tigu hermanna af sínum einum kostnaði, en hersir hverr tuttugu menn. En svá mikit hafði Haraldr konungr aukit álög ok landskyldir, at jarlar hans höfðu meira ríki en konungar höfðu fyrrum. En er þetta spurðisk um Þrándheim, þá sóttu til Haralds konungs margir ríkismenn ok gerðusk hans menn.' (Aðalbjarnarson, 1979; 98) [Wherever King Harald gained power he made it the law that all ancestral lands and possessions belonged to him; also, that all farmers had to pay a tax to him, both great and humble. He appointed an earl for every district, whose duty it was to administer the law and justice and to collect fines and taxes. And the earl was to have a third of the taxes and penalties for his maintenance and other expenses. Every earl was to have under him four or more hersar, and every hersir was to have twenty marks of reveneu. Every earl was to furnish the king with sixty soldiers for his army and every hersir, twenty. But King Harald increased imposts and taxes to such an extent that his earls had greater power than kings had had before. When this was learned in the Trondheim districts, many men of influence joined the king and became his followers.'] (Sturluson, 1964; 63)

[6] See Bagge (2010: 179-82) and subsequent references, particularly to Helle (2001), for a fuller discussion of *Heimskringla*'s inaccuracy here.

[7] For a fuller discussion of the complexity of the Christianisation process see Abrams (2000).

Works Cited

Abrams, Lesley. 'Conversion and Assimilation.' *Cultures in Contact: Scandinavian Settlement in England in the Ninth and Tenth Centuries.* Eds Dawn M. Hadley and Julian D. Richards. Turnhout: Brepols Publishers, 2000, 135-153.

Bagge, Sverre. *From Viking Stronghold to Christian Kingdom.* Copenhagen: Museum Tusculanum Press, 2010.

Bagge, Sverre. *Society and Politics in Snorri Sturluson's Heimskringla.* Berkeley: University of California Press, 1991.

Brink, Stefan. 'Law and Society: Polities and Legal Customs in Viking Scandinavia.' *The Viking World.* Eds Stefan Brink and Neil Price. London: Routledge, 2007. 23-31.

Dørum, Knut. 'The Sagas and the Reversed Retrospective Method.' *Scandinavian Journal of History.* 34.2, 2009, 205-7.

Gelting, Michael H. 'The Problem of Danish 'Feudalism'. *Feudalism: New Landscapes of Debate.* Eds Sverre Bagge, Michael H. Gelting, and Thomas Lindkvist. Turnhout: Brepols, 2011, 159-84.

Harris, Jospeh. 'Saga as Historical Novel' *Structure and Meaning in Old Norse Literature.* Eds John Lindow, Lars Lönnroth and Gard Wolfgang Weber. Odense: Odense University Press, 1986, 187-219.

Heimskringla. Ed. Bjarni Aðalbjarnarson. Reykjavík: Íslenzk Fornrit, 1979.

Hollander, Lee M. 'Introduction.' *Heimskringla. Snorri Sturluson.* Austin: University of Texas Press, 1964.

Lönnroth, Lars. 'Rhetorical Persuasion in the Sagas.' *Scandinavian Studies.* 42.2, 1970, 157-89.

Moreland, John. *Archaeology and Text.* London: Duckworth, 2003.

Myrberg, Nanouschka. 'Room for All? Spaces and Places for Thing Assemblies: The Case of the All-thing on Gotland, Sweden.' *Viking and Medieval Scandinavia*. Vol. 4, 2008, 133-57.

Orning, Hans Jacob. 'Saga and Society.' *Scandinavian Journal of History*. Vol. 33.3, 2008): 289-99.

Orning, Hans Jacob. *Unpredictability and Presence: Norwegian Kingship in the High Middle Ages*. Liden: Brill, 2007.

Richards, Julian D. *The Vikings: A Very Short Introduction*. New York: Oxford University Press. 2005.

Sanmark, Alexandra and Semple, Sarah J. 'Places of Assembly: New Discoveries in Sweden and England.' *Fornvännen*. Vol. 103, 2008, 245-259.

Sanmark, Alexandria. 'Administrative Organisation and State Formation: A Case Study of Assembly Sites in Sodermanland, Sweden.' *Medieval Archaeology*. Vol. 53, 2009, 205-241.

Sturluson, Snorri. *Heimskringla*. Trans. Lee M. Hollander. Austin: University of Texas Press, 1964.

The Earliest Norwegian Laws. Ed. L. M. Larson. New York: Columbia University Press. 1935.

Thurston, Tina L. *Landscapes of Power, Landscapes of Conflict: State Formation in the South Scandinavian Iron Age*. Dordrecht: Springer. 2002.

Landscapes of War and Vistas of Peace in 'Margareta Fredkulla' by Selma Lagerlöf

Victoria Ralph
University College London

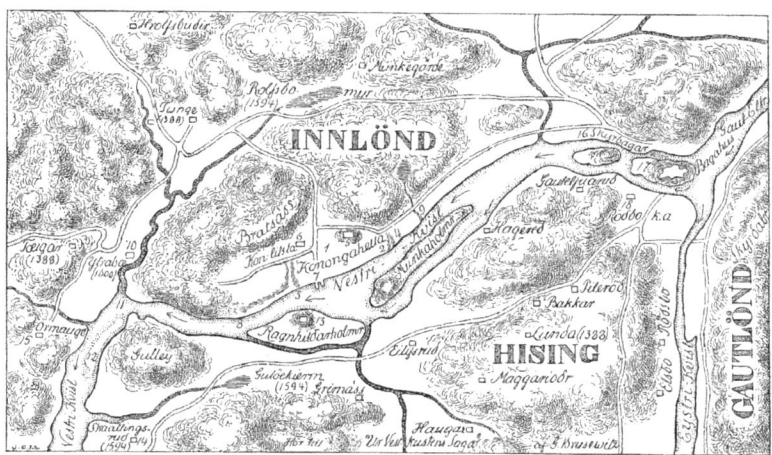

Map of Kungahälla, taken from Gustaf Brusewitz's *Ur Bohuslän's Konunga-Sagor* (1898).

'Margareta Fredkulla' is a short story in *Drottningar i Kungahälla* (1899; *The Queens of Kungahälla*, 1930) by the Swedish author Selma Lagerlöf (1858-1940) who wrote sixteen novels and seven volumes of short stories and became the first woman to win the Nobel Prize for Literature in 1909. Her Old Norse inspired works include the two-volume novel *Jerusalem* (1901-2), located to the province of Dalarna and Jerusalem, and a number of short stories (including *Drottningar i Kungahälla*) set in Bohuslän.

Drottningar i Kungahälla comprises an introduction entitled *På Det Stora Kungahällas Grund* and five short stories about different types of women in order of sequence: 'Skogsdrottningen' (savage), 'Sigrid Storråda' (valkyrie), 'Astrid' (slave), 'Margareta Fredkulla' (peace-woman) and 'Drottningen På Ragnhildsholmen' (queen). 'Margareta Fredkulla' (peace-woman) was originally written in prose but replaced with a narrative verse version in the 1933 edition.

The short story collection is located in Kungälv on the border of the west coast of Sweden in southern Bohuslän, which was once part of Norway. *På Det Stora Kungahällas Grund* charts a lost space where there are no remains to be found of the splendours of medieval Kungahälla (known as Konungahella in *Heimskringla*) that lay at the mouth of the Göta älv (known as the Gaut Elf River in *Heimskringla*) where Sigurd Jorsalafarer, the Norwegian Crusader King, built his royal castle and put a splinter of the Holy Cross in the Church to protect the land. The meeting place for the kings of Sweden, Denmark, and Norway and site of wars, peace summits and marriage unions has disappeared and been replaced by a Swedish rural idyll of a manor house surrounded by green trees and red barns.

Drottningar i Kungahälla is partially based on *Heimskringla* by Snorri Sturluson (1179-1241), which consists of fifteen sagas of Norwegian kings in order of historical sequence with *Ynglinga saga* tracing their legendary past.[1] Snorri's history relates the construction of medieval Norway as a male activity through the reporting of wars, battles, and political and historical events. With the exceptions of some powerful queens, few women are mentioned, except in subordinate roles.

This paper concentrates on the prose version of 'Margareta Fredkulla' in the original edition of *Drottningar i kungahälla*. It discusses how Lagerlöf retells the narratives of landscapes of war and conquest in Magnúss saga Berfoetts in Heimskringla to imagine vistas of peace as part of the construction of a Swedish national identity.

In *Magnúss saga Berfoetts*, Snorri relates that King Magnús laid claim to and invaded Västergötland (known as West Gautland in *Heimskringla*) with a large and well-equipped army and constructed a fort where he installed a garrison of 360 men on the island of Kvalthinsey on Lake Vänern (known as Lake Vænir in *Heimskringla*). The Norwegian King harried and burned far and wide in the forest settlements and forced the people who were subject to the Swedish king to swear him allegiance. When ice formed on Lake Vänern, King Ingi of Sweden rode down with a large army of 3,600 men and twice asked the Norwegians to depart from the fort before an attack was made. After the Norwegian garrison surrendered and returned to Norway, the people of the forest districts swapped their allegiance back again to King Ingi. However, King Magnús invaded again when the ice broke up in spring and harried and burned everywhere in the Swedish realm until he was finally defeated in battle at Foxerni by a Gautish army and fled back to Norway.

After these conflicts, Margrét Ingadóttir was betrothed in an arranged marriage to seal a peace treaty between three warring Scandinavian kings, King Magnús of Norway, King Ingi of Sweden and King Eirík of Denmark, that was signed at Kungahälla circa 1110. In *Magnúss saga Berfoetts*, Margrét is hardly given more narrative space than a mention of her name. Snorri relates that King Magnús was to obtain in marriage Margrét, the daughter of King Ingi – she was thereafter called Peace Woman – and that she was sent west from Sweden to Norway with a magnificent following. As a guarantee of reconciliation in a discourse of war, Margrét could be regarded as a peace-trophy wife. In 'Consent in Marriage: Old Norse Law, Life and Litertaure' Jochens explains that the Kings' Sagas 'portray a wide option of marriage arrangements reflecting the authors' attempts to create a credible picture of history' including examples of *herfang* (the woman being taken as booty in war or ordered by the man to come to his bed), legal procedures of *festar* (betrothals), *brúðlaup* (the wedding), and the keeping of concubines by kings and chieftains while entering into marriage in the Christian period (1986: 151). She discusses the passive role of women in marriages arranged by male relatives in which they had no say and refers to Margrét Ingadóttir as 'a glimpse of a woman who was moved like a pawn from her immediate to her marital family, a transition that often entailed a new life among former enemies' (ibid. 152).

(Her)story

In 'Margareta Fredkulla', Lagerlöf uses one of the five narrative strategies identified by Susan Brantly in historical fiction written by women 'to write a history of women in counterpoint to the history of men' (2004: 144). Lagerlöf tells the previously untold story of a woman who has been effectively silenced in Snorri's history and who is being forced into an arranged marriage against her will. Events are rewritten and seen through the eyes of the Peace Woman herself. However, Lagerlöf presents not just (her)story but (their)story, the victims of war, the people of the forest settlements who were caught up in a conflict over boundary lands.

Lagerlöf's story is set in the aftermath of a conflict over boundary lands in the burnt-down village of Storgård in Västergötland in Sweden, which lies on the southern bank of the Göta älv a little above Kungahälla. The river is regarded as the boundary between the realms of the Swedish and Norwegian kings and its source is Lake Vänern, the largest lake in Sweden. The Göta älv divides into a second branch, the Nordre älv, and they both flow into an estuary separated from the mainland by the island of Hisingen.

Snorri's brief account of Margrét's journey west from Sweden to Norway with a magnificent following is built on by Lagerlöf who imagines the details that he left out. Her Fredkulla wears a crown and a long, silken veil woven with gold as she rides through the forest in chivalric splendour on a great black horse with purple coverings and large plumes followed by a retinue of noble ladies and lords into the saga landscapes of war. The peace treaty in which Fredkulla had been betrothed to King Magnús had been signed the summer after the events that had reduced the village of Storgård to mostly blackened plots of ground where no one had dared to build new houses for fear of another war.

The full misery and devestation endured by the frontier peasants is conveyed in a narrative influenced by folktale, which communicates the tragedy of war through the perspectives of comic characters. For example, Rasmus kolargosse spreads the news of the arrival of the Princess and Per smed pinches his ear to silence him. He urges the boy not to play jests with the poor peasants who live on the frontier when the kings of the North do not keep peace. Per smed feels frightened of what the peasants who are flocking to the village might do if they were beguiled into false hopes of peace and blames the enchantments of a wood fairy, *skogsrå*. He insists that the *skogsrå* has transformed herself into a Princess because she knows that last summer at Kungahälla King Inge had a meeting with the Norwegian King Magnus to treat about peace. The fairy-tale image could have been inspired by Viktor Rydberg's poem 'Skogsrået' in *Dikter* (1882). The full horror of an enemy unexpectedly arriving on the doorstep in the middle of the night is emphasised in Sigrid Torsdotter's predictions that the shapes of warriors in her hearth-fire signify another attack. She makes the people shudder with fear as she warns that people will wake up, half-choked, in their smoke-filled cottages while the Norwegian King's men raise their cry of victory before the burning walls.

Fredkulla's eyes filled with tears when she arrives in the village of Storgård as she looked at the blackened sites, the pillaged houses, and the barbarised people. She has never before seen so much misery and she makes a vow to be an instrument of peace out of a spirit of compassion for the sake of a war-ravaged people, though she senses that it could cost her her own happiness and life.

> Det vill jag, att i alla skolen minnas vad jag nu lovar vid Gud och alla helgon: Så länge som jag äger ord på tungan, så länge som jag äger blod i hjärtat, så länge skall jag verka fredens verk. (Lagerlöf, 1911: 115)

> 'I wish you all to remember the vow I now take before God and all His saints. So long as I have words on my tongue, so long as I have blood in my heart, I will devote myself to the work of peace. (trans. C Field, 1930: 170)

The setting of the three-cornered market-place in the burnt-down village of Storgård where three roads meets becomes the folktale counterpart of the traditional meeting place in Kungahälla for the three kings of Norway, Sweden, and Denmark in *Heimskringla*.

Lagerlöf retells an erotic episode that is included in P.A. Munch's 1859 Norwegian translation of *Heimskringla*.[2] The love poetry attributed to King Magnus and composed for Mathilda, the Emperor's Daughter in the East with whom he is so smitten that he has sleepless nights is summarised into prose in Munch's version but reinterpreted poetically by Lagerlöf.

En är hon, som mig binder
att vaka långa nätter,
en är, som mig förmenar
att njuta lek och fröjder,
den fagra mön i östern,
som själv sitt rike värjer,
svarthårig, svartögd stridsmås
Matilda, kejsarns dotter.

(Lagerlöf, 1911:116).

There is one who me compelleth
Day and night on her to muse,
All my other joys she killeth,
All their coaxings I refuse.
Black her tresses, and she smiteth
With her black eyes like a spear;
Peerless, she my heart delighteth,
She, the Emperor's daughter dear.

(trans. C. Field, 1930: 171)

When a little shepherd boy sings two verses of this love poetry, Fredkulla shows great distress at being forced to marry a man who obviously doesn't love her. Lagerlöf's narrative is tongue-in-cheek, the concept of love taking over a discourse of war through the narrative medium of medieval chivalric romance is subtly reversed as the first verse is addressed to a *stridsmås*. This could be Lagerlöf's allusion to Matilda of Tuscany, a contemporary of King Magnús, noted for her military achievements, who embodies the image of an Old Norse warrior woman and would appear to be an ideal love-match for the warlike King. This poetic episode highlights the effect of a psychologically probing narrative in which Lagerlöf is attributing the imagined thoughts, feelings and attitudes to love and marriage from a later Christian time period to her pagan heroine. Jochens (1986) points out that although the notion of Christian consent was introduced in the North just before the end of the twelfth century, in the Kings' Sagas, it was applied to narratives from the end of the tenth century anachronistically. Lagerlöf's retelling mirrors the intermingling of pagan and Christian ideas in the King's Sagas. She does, however, omit Snorri's listing of the names of King Magnús's three sons by different mothers, one of whom was his mistress.

Lagerlöf's heroine is so afraid of the sacrifice that is demanded of her that she tries to ride back home. When she turns back out of love for the great beauty of peace, she shows that she doesn´t bear her name in vain. She earns such reverence from the people that they whisper to one another that no one should praise her deed (an indirect critical reference to the role of skaldic poetry to enhance the image of the conquering King in *Heimskringla*).

As Fredkulla crosses the Göta älv, the external border between Sweden and Norway, by ferry, she looks down at the water and sees the gentle waves that flow unrelentingly to the sea, not hesitating to cast themselves into the embrace of the strong ocean. She talks to herself and sees her own destiny as a gentle wave that must go onward into the world's tumult to modify its bitterness. The watery imagery suits Kungahälla's estuary setting, which is subject to the moods and swings of several currents from the river and the ocean and the sea. In Margaret Cohen's 'Chronotopes of the Sea' the brown water of the river 'gives elemental form to the tension between origins and outreach as it connects the earth of home and the great waters of the wide world in its linear flow' (2006: 225). The personification of Fredkulla as a gentle wave and the repetition of feminine pronouns in the passage combine the feminine element of water with a symbol of national identity as the earth of Sweden is carried along the current of the Göta älv from its peaceful source of Lake Vänern. The construction of a Norwegian fort on Lake Vänern by King Magnús in *Heimskringla* could be interpreted as an attempt to subjugate the feminine element of water in the landscape that represents a Swedish source of peace.

On the other side of the river, war and peace confront one another as Fredkulla comes face to face with an enemy she must marry. In a passage that resounds with masculine pronouns, the suspense and danger are heightened as King Magnus rides towards her. Lagerlöf appropriates Snorri's magnificent descriptions of the outward appearance of the warlike King. Fredkulla sees his long, silken blond hair waving on his shoulders. She sees his crest of the golden lion on his helmet, the banner above him that is blazoned on his red silken garments and his proud bearing. Earlier in the story, the peasants' wives had told the Peace Woman not to think of their sorrows but to think of King Magnus, the noble hero to whom she belongs and to stroke in fancy his long, blond, silky hair. However, any attractions that a young maiden may have romantically felt for a handsome King have been shattered on her bridal journey when she saw the results of Viking brutality. Lagerlöf criticises the nineteenth century romanticised image of the Viking hero and his glorious deeds with her predatory metaphor of King Magnus as a beast, the Lion of the North as King of the Jungle with a warlike look in his eyes. As King Magnus rides towards Fredkulla, he casts a black shadow over the fields in the evening sunlight and she thinks she would rather throw herself beneath the hooves of his galloping horse than marry him.

Conclusion

In *Atlas of the European Novel* 1800-1900, Franco Moretti points out that historical novels in nineteenth century Europe were situated away from the centre to the border, reflecting the concerns of the age of National Romanticism when national borders were being consolidated (1999: 33-5). *Drottningar i Kungahälla* could be interpreted as incorporating a peripheral region into the larger unit of Sweden and reflecting a process that was taking place socially and politically. Bohuslän, with its strategic position, had been the site of border wars for centuries before the province was finally ceded to Sweden in the Peace of Roskilde in 1658. However, it continued to be regarded as a 'Norwegian' province where the people spoke Norwegian. It gradually became more 'Swedish' during the nineteenth century, when its people were taught to speak Swedish with the introduction of compulsory schooling and with the increased popularity of its seaside health resort areas.

Drottningar i Kungahälla arises from an exploration of local and national history, archaeology, mythology, folklore, the Viking Age heritage, and Old Norse literature that were part of a national consciousness raising process. It was partially based on *Heimskringla*, an iconic text in nineteenth century Scandinavia, but an exclusive bible of Norwegian nationalism. The stories in the collection re-assert 'Swedish' claims to a shared Old-Norse heritage, a message that would have been understood by Lagerlöf's contemporaries when it was published in 1899, in the run up to the dissolution of the Swedish-Norwegian Union of Crowns in 1905.

In 'Margareta Fredkulla', the narratives of landscapes of war and conquest in *Heimskringla* are seen from a woman's perspective and revealed as sites of senseless suffering and charred destruction. Lagerlöf imagines a positive and active role in history with a dialogue of peace for a Swedish woman caught up in a Norwegian discourse of war and male power. In this story, which pre-dates Lagerlöf's later pacifist novel *Bannlyst* (*The Outcast*) published at the end of the First World War in 1918, the message of peace is embodied in the image of the Peace Woman, who is aligned with the 'vistas of peace' located in Lake Vänern. Margareta Fredkulla becomes a Swedish national symbol of peace as part of the construction of a Swedish national identity that incorporates a pacifist ideal.

Notes

[1] Selma Lagerlöf could also have used the Swedish translation of Heimskringla by H.O. Hildebrand (1869-1871).

[2] Munch's Norwegian translation of Snorri's Heimskringla includes apochryphal material and contains additional narratives from other Kings' Sagas, for example, pættir or tales from Morkinskinna.

Works Cited

Anderson, Benedict. *Imagined Communities. Reflections on the Origin and Spread of Nationalism*. London, New York: Verso, 1991.

Brantly, Susan. 'Gender and the Historical Novel.' *Gender-Power-Text: Nordic Culture In the Twentieth Century*. Ed. Helena Forsås-Scott. London: Norvik Press, 2004, 139-153.

Cohen, Margaret. 'The Chronotopoes of the Sea.' *The Novel, Vol. 2: Forms and Themes*. Ed. Franco Moretti. Princeton, Oxford: Princeton University Press, 2006, 647-666.

Hildebrand, Hans. *Konungasagor: sagor om ynglingarne och Norges Konungar intill 1177 af Snorre Sturleson*. Stockholm: Beijers Förlag, 1869.

Jochens, Jenny, M. 'Consent In Marriage: Old Norse, Law, Life and Literture.' *Scandinavian Studies* 58, 1986, 142-176.

Jones, Michael and Olwig, Kenneth. *Nordic Landscapes*. Minnesota, London: University Of Minnesota Press, 2008.

Kress, Helga. 'Flæði í Laxdælu: Haf og Skegg.' *Óþarfur Unnustur og aðrar greinar um íslenskar bókmenntir*. Ed. Gunnþórunn Guðmundsdóttir. Reykjavík: Bókmennta og listfræðastofnun, Háskóli Íslands, 2009, 30-43.

Lagerlöf, Selma. *Drottningar i Kungahälla*. Stockholm: A. Bonniers, 1910.

---. *Drottningar i Kungahälla*, sjunde upplagan, Stockholm, Albert Bonniers Förlag, 1911.

Lagerlöf, Selma, *The Queens of Kungahälla*. Trans. C. Field. London: T Werner Laurie, 1930.

Lagerroth, Erland. 'The Narrative Art of Selma Lagerlöf: Two Problems.' *Scandinavian Studies* 33:1, 1961, 10-17.

Lagerroth, Erland. *Selma Lagerlöf Och Bohuslän, En studie i hennes 90-talsdiktning*. Lund: Gleerups Förlag, 1963.

McDowell, Linda. 'Place and Space.' *A Concise Companion to Feminist Theory*. Ed. Mary Eagleton. Malden, MA: Blackwell, 2003, 11-31.

Moretti, Franco. *Atlas of the European Novel, 1800-1900*. London, New York: Verso, 1999.

Moretti, Franco. *Graphs, Maps, Trees*: Abstract Models for Literary History. London: Verso, 2005.

Morkinskinna: The Earliest Icelandic Chronicle of the Norwegian Kings (1030-1157) Islandica Vol. LI. Trans. Theodore M. Andersson and Kari Ellen Gade. Ithaca and London: Cornell University Press, 2000.

Rydberg, Viktor, *Dikter*. 1882. Stockholm: Bonnier, 1930.

Sturluson, Snorri. *Heimskringla: History of the Kings of Norway*. Trans. Lee M. Hollander. Austin: Texas University Press, 1964.

Sturluson, Snorri. *Norges konge-sager fra de ældste tider indtil anden halvdeel af det 13de aarundrede efter Christi Fødsel/forfattede af Snorre Sturlassøn, Sturla Thordssøon og flere*. Trans. P.A. Munch. Christiania: W C Fabritius og G E Pettersen, 1859-1871.

'The History of Bohuslän.' *Sverige Turism*. 9 February 2014. <http://www.sverigeturism.se/smorgasbord/index.html>

Thomsen, Bjarne Thorup. '(Trans)national Geographies and Alternative Families in Selma Lagerlöf's Bannlyst.' *European Journal of Scandinavian Studies* 42.1 (2012): 1-18.

Wawn, Andrew, ed. Northern Antiquity: *The Post-Medieval Reception of Edda and Saga*. Enfield Lock, Middlesex: Hisarlik Press, 1994.

The Fårö Documents: The Political or Regionalised Ingmar Bergman?

Ian Giles
The University of Edinburgh

The Fårö Documents are two documentaries produced for television by director Ingmar Bergman in 1969 and 1979 respectively. Since their respective premieres some thirty and forty years ago, the films have been fairly neglected by Bergman scholars.[1] This paper seeks to present these documentaries, which are so untypical of Bergman's oeuvre, to a wider audience and establish how they reflect Ingmar Bergman's political interests and his developing involvement in regionalism as a newly-arrived inhabitant of Fårö.

Secondary sources disagree about the precise titles of the two films, in particular the spelling of *dokument*/document, but those used for the DVD releases seem a fair compromise. These are, respectively, *Fårö Dokument* and *Fårö Dokument 1979*. In order to avoid ambiguity when discussing these two films, they will be referred to as *FD69* and *FD79*.

In his autobiography, Ingmar Bergman describes his determination to shoot his 1961 film *Through a Glass Darkly* in Orkney and his producer's desperation to avoid an expensive foreign shoot. As a last resort, Bergman was dispatched to the island of Fårö off the northern coast of Gotland one stormy day in April to carry out reconnaissance for the shoot. He describes how he immediately fell in love with the island: 'I told Sven Nykvist I wanted to live on the island for the rest of my life'

(Bergman, 1988: 207-8). Bergman did not expand on his feelings for Fårö on any single occasion, but his remarks over the years do provide some insight into his relationship with the island. He told Röster i Radio-TV in 1970: 'The reality of Fårö has had a stabilising impact on me and my work. By living in a reality I understand and whose proportions I can grasp, I can gain better insight into what happens outside it' (Steene, 2005: 419).

Bergman moved to Fårö permanently in 1966 and described the life he led there as one that cleansed his soul, stating that 'after a month or two I was hopelessly involved in the islanders' problems', which resulted in the production of *FD69* (Bergman, 1988: 208). Indeed, Fårö became an anchor in Bergman's life after his relocation to the island and a place to which he would regularly turn in times of crisis.[2]

One of the first public indications that Bergman was interested in making a documentary was an interview at Råsunda in February 1969. He told Stig Björkman about his possible future film projects: 'When I get back to Fårö I'm going to make a film about sheep-rearing. The idea has gradually grown on me to document Fårö, in short films lasting a couple of minutes or so. No large scale profundities; just ten, fifteen, twenty short films' (Björkman et al., 1973: 249).

The filming of *FD69* commenced on the 15th of March 1969 and was completed some 6 weeks later on the 1st of May. The crew consisted of just five people working out of a single caravan;[3] most crucially Bergman himself as director, his ever-present right hand man Sven Nykvist as cinematographer and Arne Carlsson as soundman (Steene, 2005: 419). The film focuses on a handful of Fårö-natives, primarily through interviews conducted in a domestic setting or while otherwise engaged in their respective occupations. Bergman, aside from directing, acts as interviewer as well as narrator and advocate through the voiceover.

FD79 was conceived in the summer of 1976, when Bergman spent six weeks at his house on Fårö. He and Arne Carlsson, Bergman's long-standing stills photographer, and the soundman on *FD69*, began to define the outlines of a follow-up film ('Fårö Document 1979'). It was Carlsson's suggestion to contrast the tourist-packed Fårö resort of Sudersand with the island's emptiness the rest of the year. Bergman commented: 'Arne and I both thought that the schizophrenia surrounding Fårö was something worth documenting' ('Fårö Document 1979').

A more drawn-out affair than the making of *FD69*, the filming of *FD79* was done over three years, with Arne Carlsson responsible for much of the photography during the period, as Bergman was in self-imposed exile from Sweden. The interview segments were all recorded in 1979. The film, in a similar manner to *FD69*, observes various islanders engaged in their day-to-day activities. There is, however, far more emphasis on observation than on the keen interviewing that characterised *FD69*. In all probability, this was the result of a final cut almost twice as long as *FD69*, taken from 44 hours of footage ('Fårö Document 1979').

The contrast between the two films is marked. Bergman's influence on *FD69* is apparent as the documentary moves swiftly from scene to scene, bearing many of the traits of Bergmanian films[4] and emphasising the director as reporter, highlighting the political issues at hand. In contrast, *FD79* is the result of Bergman sifting through Arne Carlsson's footage in the cutting room, which led to a far more languid pace, showing off the regional scenery rather than making a fast impact on the audience.

Many of Bergman's works have premiered at significant times of year, with the clear intention of maximising exposure for the films. A great many films have enjoyed premieres in December, close to the Christmas and New Year holidays.[5] *FD69* and *FD79*

Author and Self-Image

were no different in this respect; Bergman's cachet ensured his semi-political work was watched by a wide audience.

FD69 was first broadcast on Sweden's TV1 on the 1st of January 1970 in an 88 minute cut ('Fårö Document'). According to Steene, this was watched by millions of viewers (Steene, 2005: 419). It was aired a second time in 1970 on TV1 on March 27th as a 57 minute cut ('Fårö Document'); this is the cut available today. It is very likely that FD69 was one of the televisual highlights of the Swedish festive season of 1969/70 and that it enjoyed far greater exposure than any of Bergman's feature films on cinematic release.

Despite some doubts about the exact date of the original broadcast of FD79, we know that it took place during the Christmas holidays of that year, and that it had a running time of 103 minutes.6 Regardless of the exact date, FD79 would have been watched by hundreds of thousands, if not millions, of viewers.

It is particularly interesting to note the range of responses to the two documentaries. In Sweden, FD69 was a critical success. It was received by the critics and the audience at large as the emergence of Bergman as a concerned citizen standing up for a tiny and marginalised minority. Mauritz Edström, reviewing FD69 for Swedish daily newspaper *Dagens Nyheter* remarked: 'In my opinion, Ingmar Bergman's documentary about Fårö definitely ranks among his best films. Not thanks to any remarkable stylistic devices: on the contrary – because it was so straightforward and close to its subject' (cited in 'Fårö Document').

International critics were not so generous in their response to the film, with *Variety*'s response summarised by the following: '[t]he subject is too provincial even for persons interested in film-making as a whole' (Cited by Steene, 2005: 419).

The clear contrast between domestic and international critics is alluded to by *Variety* in their description of the film as 'provincial'. The Swedish appreciation (and occasional lack thereof) for the film was based upon Bergman's articulate political interest in a regional issue. For many amongst the Swedish public, the documentary must have diverged significantly from what they would have come to expect from Bergman. On the other hand, without an understanding for the regionalised context of *FD69*, and quite probably little-to-no knowledge of Bergman's emphatic non-involvement in politics, foreign observers must have been mystified as to why so much time was dedicated to interviewing farmers and librarians.

FD79 was more widely reviewed and written about than *FD69*. Domestically, the response was more widespread and somewhat more favourable. Elisabeth Sörensen's review for *Svenska Dagbladet* epitomises the positive reviews from within Sweden: 'Bergman has created a document of the times – the landscape lends it an eternal perspective. Just look at the image of Fårösund drenched in the sprat of a spring storm! A drama that no dramatist could accomplish' (cited in 'Fårö Document 1979').

The view from abroad was less clear-cut. Phillip Strick exemplifies how many viewed Bergman with his comment that the director's depiction of pig slaughter was a return to form (Strick, 1981: 176). Janet Maslin of the *New York Times* rather poignantly elaborated on something that no Swedish critic had picked up on: 'A t-shirt worn casually by one farmer's wife, with a 'Faro' logo, says more about the island's popularity than anything Mr. Bergman cares to say. It's too bad he doesn't address his own impact upon the place' (Maslin, 1980). It was reported that the response to the documentary in France had been that it was '[b]oring and only suitable for real "fanatics"' (*Göteborgsposten* cited by 'Fårödokument 1979', my translation).

In the case of *FD79*, the negative sentiment was not solely restricted to international reviewers. While it might be argued that regional issues were capable of drawing the public's interest, the notion of a regionalised minority also worked the other way around. *Norrländska Socialdemokraten* wrote: 'The inhabitants complained that they were marginalised by the authorities of the larger municipality covering all of Gotland. They believed the municipality had become too large. 3000 sq/km is too much, according to them. Figures like that are nothing unusual to us up here in the north. Who really thinks that Boden, for example, is a particularly large municipality? In reality, Boden is 50% larger than Gotland' (cited in'Fårödokument 1979', my translation).

Likewise, a letter writer to the same newspaper complained that the documentary had been a waste of license payers' money because of Bergman's politicisation of an unimportant regional issue, replete with stereotypes all kinds, which could only ever be of use in the teaching of history to school children (cited in 'Fårödokument 1979').

Many Bergman biographers and critics have chosen to describe *FD69* and *FD79* as 'political' in nature. This is understandable to an audience that has seen both films, particularly given the strength of their respective conclusions – and was clearly the response of many contemporary critics. However, Bergman did not agree with this sentiment, and was rather dismissive when questioned about it in 1970, in the aftermath of *FD69*. Bergman explained that his hard-hitting concluding message in the film had been written very early on in the production process.

> Jones Sima: So your political attitude to your material was clear from the outset?
> Ingmar Bergman: Whether it was political I couldn't say. After I'd been working on the film a few weeks, it just crystallized

of its own accord. I felt they were living under humiliating conditions. (Björkman et al., 1973: 264-65)

Within that statement, Bergman is clear that it is the people of Fårö for whom he cares, not the political situation. In his view, any political discourse that can be distilled from *FD69* is merely a perception. Bergman saw *FD69* as a means to an end: a method of increasing awareness of Fårö and improving life on the island.

Bergman was never questioned about the political nature of *FD79*. However, as has already been noted, the film was produced during Bergman's exile from Sweden. Indeed, *FD79* appears to be less of an overview of the state of the island and more of a declaration of love to the island and its people (Elisabeth Sörenson cited by 'Fårö Document 1979'). This transforms the documentary from a statement of a political nature made by a political exile into one of heartfelt regionalism made by a smitten immigrant to the island.

Because of Bergman's reluctance to state on record whether the films were intended as commentaries, whether political or regional, it is necessary to look elsewhere in an attempt to ascertain which purpose they were intended to serve, with a particular focus on their critical reception being key. Swedish critics such as Edström and Sörensen saw the Fårö documents as a change of focus for Bergman: from successful movie director to concerned citizen. It is clear that they regard the totality of the documentaries as a conscious cinematic choice by Bergman and consequently as a political declaration. Other critics, such as the previously cited letter writer in the north of Sweden, seem to concur. This domestic response must have been due in part to an awareness in Sweden of Bergman as an ordinarily non-political public figure, which is why the documentaries caused such strong critical reactions, positive and negative alike. In contrast, the negativity towards the films from international critics was often due to their perception that little happened in what were thematically and stylistically dull films, with critics seeming to have limited empathy for the context of Fårö. In spite of this, several foreign critics, like Maslin, clearly had a brief to review the documentaries as political works. This poses an interesting but unanswered question upon which we can merely speculate: if Bergman denied the political elements of the films, yet the audience chose to interpret them as such, were the directorial decisions he made during filming and in the cutting room politically motivated? Without access to the frank views of the late Bergman, this may be impossible to determine, making it necessary instead to defer to the summative view of the critical response, which regarded the documentaries as films about implied political issues in a regional context.

Bergman's approach to the political question of Fårö can perhaps best be understood by examining his views on politics, which are beautifully summarised in his autobiography when he relates his inner torment after the Holocaust had come to light at the end of the Second World War: '[p]olitics – never again! Of course, I should have made an utterly different decision' (Bergman, 1988: 124). While it can be supposed that Bergman regretted not being more politically active, he appears to have approached the Fårö documentaries not just as film projects, nor the documentation of society, but as a political activity. However, just as with Bergman in life, politics in the films often lay just beneath the surface in his questioning. It is the interviewee who, as often as not, provides the political statement. Bergman's political act was to be complicit in this. In the case of many of the beach resort scenes, it was left entirely to the audience's discretion to determine how political, or not, the scenes were. Indeed, as in life, politics only slips out into the open very briefly in the documentaries: during their respective concluding voiceover narratives. Bergman was very logical in his manner: he laid out the political failures; he laid out the manner in which they could be resolved; then he stepped away from the debate for ten years. This can in many ways be likened to one of Bergman's other rare political moments, when he chose to leave Sweden after being investigated by the tax authorities.

One area that needs further examination is why a follow up documentary was never produced. In the conclusion of *FD79*, Bergman expresses his desire to make a sequel in 1989, but this never happened. The obvious reason is that Bergman withdrew from film making after *Fanny and Alexander* in 1982. However, he did continue to work, producing content for television and theatre. Arguably, given his view that his documentary work would have no impact upon his feature films, it would not be unreasonable to assume that he could have been happy to work on a third Fårö Document. Bergman's involvement in the 1987 documentary *Gotska Sandön* makes the absence of a *FD89* all the more noteworthy. Materials in the Bergman archives might plausibly shed light on why a third documentary film was never produced.

As highlighted above, another crucial area for further research would be the examination of the long lost film *Gotska Sandön*, which was directed by Arne Carlsson but produced and edited by Bergman himself in 1987. The film is a portrait of the lives of people living on the isolated Baltic island of Gotska Sandön, at a time when the population was dwindling rapidly.[7] It would be particularly interesting to establish whether there are similarities in composition between *FD79* and *Gotska Sandön*, as it might be helpful in determining more precisely the role played by Bergman in the making of *FD79*. Hopefully, this will soon be possible, as the film was shown for the first time in many years during the September 2011 *Fårönatta* festival on Fårö and has been screened a handful of times subsequently.

Mauritz Edström remarked upon reviewing *FD79* that he was 'convinced that these films will continue to stand as documents longer even than many of Bergman's other films' (cited in 'Fårö Document 1979'). What do these films show? Do they show a politicised or regionalised Bergman, or do they merely show a Bergman in love with his new home? Evidently, Bergman took these 'side projects' just as seriously as his feature films and closer examination of them by scholars of Bergman would undoubtedly shed further light on the cinematic director as a political individual. However, the political aspect of the documentaries, noted by lay audiences and critics alike, was entirely reliant on regional context. Political issues were the foundation that ensured the Fårö Documents were strong documentary films, and very much a sign of Bergman's love for his adopted home. Without these, Bergman would surely not have been interested in making the films at all. The question of whether Bergman was political or regionalised can only be resolved through an acknowlegement of the complex relationship between these two concepts and the specific context that formed the genesis for the films. In the fullness of time, the words of Edström may be realised, allowing the Fårö Documents to stand once again as testaments to Bergman's life and work on Fårö, whether that is in a personal, cinematic, political, or regional capacity.

Notes

[1] With the recent exception of Elisa Jochum's analysis of the films, also published on the Norvik Press: see Jochum, 2012.

[2] See Bergman, 1988: 95, 100, 103-04, 106 and 228 for further details.

[3] Although this somewhat romantic illusion is slightly dispelled by the fact that Bergman would presumably have returned to his home during this period, given that construction of it had been completed in 1966.

[4] Including but not limited to swift movement between scenes, framing of shots, use of sound and sound recording techniques, visual motifs, subject matter, etc.

[5] For a comprehensive overview of original premiere dates for Bergman's films see Steene, 2005.

[6] Although there is also uncertainty about the original running time, with SFI, Steene, and the Ingmar Bergman Foundation all disagreeing. For further details see Giles, 2012.

[7] Indeed, the island no longer has a permanent population, leaving Carlsson and Bergman's work as one of the final documents of island life. For further information on the island consult 'Gotska Sandön'. Gotlandnet AB. Available: < http://www.gotland.net/resa/gotska-sandon > 18 Oct. 2013.

Works Cited

'Fårö Document'. *Ingmar Bergman Foundation*. 18 Oct. 2013. <http://ingmarbergman.se/sv/production/farodokument-1166>

'The Faro Document 1969'. *Bergmanorama: The Magic Works of Ingmar Bergman*. 18 Oct. 2013. <http://bergmanorama.webs.com/films/faro_69.htm>

'Fårö Document 1979'. *Ingmar Bergman Foundation*. 18 Oct. 2013. <http://ingmarbergman.se/sv/production/farodokument-1979-1002>

'Fårödokument 1979 (1979)'. *Svensk Filmdatabas. Svenska Filminstitutet*. 18 Oct. 2013. <http://www.sfi.se/sv/svensk-filmdatabas/Item/?itemid=8733&type=MOVIE&iv=Basic%3E>

'Gotska Sandön'. *Visit Gotland. Gotlandnet AB*. 18 Oct. 2013. <http://www.gotland.net/resa/gotska-sandon>

'Gotska Sandön'. *Sudersandsbiografen*, 2013. 18 Oct. 2013. <http://sudersandsbion.se/portfolio/gotska-sandon-2/>

Fårö Document. Dir. Ingmar Bergman. Bergman Centre on Fårö Foundation, 2011.

Fårö Document 1979. Dir. Ingmar Bergman. Tartan, 2006.

Bergman, Ingmar. *Images: My Life in Film*. London: Bloomsbury, 1994.

---. *The Magic Lantern: An Autobiography*. London: Penguin, 1988.

Björkman, Stig, et al. *Bergman on Bergman: Interviews with Ingmar Bergman*. London: Secker and Warburg, 1973.

Giles, Ian. 'Perspectives on Ingmar Bergman's Fårö Documents'. Masters Essay. University of Edinburgh, 2012.

Jochum, Elisa. 'Bergman's Fårö'. *Framed Horrizons: Student Writing on Nordic Literature*. Eds Marita Fraser, et al. London: Norvik Press, 2012, 31-62.

Maslin, Janet. 'Faro Document 1979 (1979): '"Faro Document '79", a Bergman Revisitation'. *The New York Times*. 18 Oct. 2013. <http://www.nytimes.com/movie/review?res=9D06E5D61638F933A05753C1A966948260>

Steene, Birgitta. *Ingmar Bergman: A Reference Guide*. Amsterdam: Amsterdam University Press, 2005.

Strick, Philip. 'Fårö-Dokument 1979 (Fårö 1979)'. *Monthly Film Bulletin* 48.564/575, 1981, 176.

The Art of Entertaining a Nation under Nazi Occupation: Pierre Andrézel and *Gengældelsens Veje*

Barbara Tesio
University of Edinburgh

The aim of this paper is to suggest a new path in the studies of the work of Karen Blixen, intentionally using the unusual starting point of *Gengældelsens Veje* (1944, The Angelic Avengers, 1947), Blixen's only novel and least explored work. This highly controversial text, largely underrated by Blixenian scholars, contains two main deviations from her usual writing routine. Firstly, it is a novel, while her usual production is made up of short stories, and secondly, it is the only book she wrote in Danish, instead of English, her usual literary language. The focus on these two features will offer a fascinating opportunity to explore the relationship between displacement, language and identity, which characterizes Blixen's entire production.

Gengældedens Veje and its historical circumstances

When the Germans occupied Denmark in 1940, Karen Blixen found herself isolated in Rungstedlund, her childhood home into which she had permanently moved after her return from Africa. By then, she was already an affirmed writer thanks to the success of her first book *Seven Gothic Tales*, published in 1934 under the pseudonym Isak Dinesen. Twenty years before, in Kenya, she had started a coffee plantation with her husband Bror Blixen, which eventually went bankrupt. She divorced her husband a few years after they arrived in Africa. The report of her African years, the most significant and passionate of her life, is well known through her best-selling memoir *Out of Africa* (1937). Starting a career as a writer was her attempt to save herself from the depression she fell into after the death of her lover Denys Finch-Hatton, the loss of her African farm and her consequent, inevitable return to Denmark. Even if writing had become her refuge already during the most difficult period in Africa, she began to take it seriously only once she got back to Denmark in 1931 and had to face the problem of reinventing her life as a single, middle-aged woman. Robert Langbaum, in his book *Isak Dinsesen's Art*, reports the amusing story that she used to tell in order to explain the start of her writing career:

> She asked her brother Thomas to finance her for two years while she found something to do. There were only three things, she told him, she could do better than average. She could cook [...]; she could take care of mad people; she could write. They settled on writing, and she produced Seven Gothic Tales two years later. (1975: 43)

Under the Nazi occupation, connections with the rest of the world were cut off, so Blixen was unable to receive her royalties from abroad. Alone, plagued by the illness that had marked the greatest part of her life, angry with the German occupiers and frustrated with the passivity of her fellow Danes, she started to write *Gengældelsens Veje*, a Gothic thriller that she published under the French pseudonym Pierre Andrézel. To her great surprise, due the minimal effort she put into writing the novel, the book quickly became a bestseller, translated and published in several languages, and seized upon in America by The-Book-of-the-Month Club. *Gengældelsens Veje* is the only novel Karen Blixen wrote, and the only book she wrote in Danish first instead of English. It was first published in 1944 in Denmark by the countries biggest publisher, Gyldendal. The book, and the mystery surrounding its author, immediately occupied the pages of magazines and stimulated the minds of the most authoritative names of the academic world. Despite her precautions to remain hidden by the new pen name, Blixen was quickly suggested as a possible author. In an attempt to put an end to the question, she took part in the debate by publishing an article entitled "Om Pseudonymer og *Gengældelsens Veje*" in the newspaper Berlingske Aftenavis (23. November 1944) in which she firmly denied the authorship of the novel. It was only in an interview in 1956 that she publicly admitted to be the author of *Gengældelsens Veje*. In the meantime, the novel had become a huge success.

The book, set in 1840 in England and France, has been considered a pastiche of the Victorian governess novel and the Gothic novel by several scholars (Langbaum, 1975; Brix, 1949; Hannah, 1971). It tells the story of two young women, Lucan Bellenden and Zosine Tabbernor, who after a series of misfortunes end up in the grip of the Reverend Pennhallow and his wife at their farm Saint-Barbe. The old couple conceal, under a perfect façade of charity works, their main activity, sexual slavery. When Zosine and Lucan discover the truth, they decide to stay and fight back, rather than escape, and, eventually, they succeed. *Gengældelsens Veje* has mostly been considered as one of Blixen's minor works, a mere pastiche unworthy of serious academic consideration. Judith Thurman, Blixen's biographer, in *Isak Dinesen: The Life of Karen Blixen*, defines it as 'refreshingly silly' (1982: 306), while Hannah considers the book to have 'little or no value as literature' (1971: 49). Blixen herself contributed to the process of undervaluing it by constantly denying its authorship. When she finally admitted to being the author of the book, she defined it as her 'highly illegitimate child' and underlined that the book was not to be taken seriously, since it was conceived as pure entertainment for both the author and the reader (Brix, 1949: 255). However, when *Shadows on the Grass* was published in 1961, Blixen described the creative process that led her to write her only novel, suggesting some deeper implications:

> When I started on the first page of the book, I had no idea whatever was going to happen in it, it ran on upon its own and – as was probably inevitable under the circumstances – developed into a tale of darkness. But when in the summer of 1943 the German persecution of Danish Jews set in, and most homes along the coast of the Sound were housing Jewish fugitives from Copenhagen waiting to be got across to Sweden, I slackened in my work; it began to look crude and vulgar to me compete with the surrounding world in creating horrors. Also, in the following months the Danish resistance movement fetched headway, we all began to rise from our sham graves, drawing the air more freely and ceasing to gasp for breath. My life-saving book on its own put on a happy ending and – since I looked upon it as a highly illegitimate child – it was published under the pseudonym of Pierre Andrézel. (1961: 132)

Karen Blixen is here putting the emphasis on three fundamental features, namely the historical contextualisation of the text and the two consequent, and inevitably connected, ideas of a literature of encouragement and a literature of entertainment. She commences her explanation by writing that the book 'ran upon its own' because of the 'circumstances' that surrounded her. By listing some of the most important events of the difficult years of the Nazi occupation of Denmark, she reminds the reader of the exceptional and extraordinary times in which the book was conceived. Compared to her other works, *Gengældelsens Veje* is certainly different and peculiar and at first impression it would appear to diverge from her usual art. For a storyteller used to the world of short tales, the writing of a novel can appear as slightly unusual. Indeed, her feelings towards this book were always very troubled. However, this quotation is implicitly suggesting more profound interpretations that resist simply labeling the novel as a book with 'little or no value as literature'.

Storytelling

Karen Blixen established her authorial fame with the pen name Isak Dinesen, and she constantly underlined her belonging to the tradition of storytelling: 'I am not a novelist, really not even a writer; I am a storyteller' (Wilkinson, 2004: 77). As with most of her tales, *Gengældelsens Veje* is set in a distant past. One of the most frequent critiques of her first book, *Seven Gothic Tales*, when it was first published in Denmark in 1935, was that it was too distant from present times, an unacceptable sin in a time that needed art for the people and thus bound to people's present. In the middle of the Depression, the leading genre in Denmark was sociological realism, with works such as *Hans Kirke's Fiskerne* (1928) or *H.C. Branners Legetøj* (1936). As Thurman rightly underlines: '[a]mong intellectuals there was a general spirit of austerity and sympathy for the political struggles of the working class' (Thurman, 1982: 279). However, what some of Blixen's contemporary critics failed to understand, was that the reference to the past in Blixen's writing did not signal a detachment from reality, but rather a search for models that could be used in order to enlighten a difficult present situation. And the role of the storyteller is to explain and remind her people of such models.

The fundamental concept in Isak Dinesen's writing technique is distancing. What a good storyteller does is 'to tell tales in order to delight the world and make it wiser,' as Mira Jama – the character that in her narrative world represents the storyteller par excellence – says (Dinesen, 1957: 12). The best way to do this is to create enough distance from the story by setting it in an ideal past. Setting the tale in the past gives both the storyteller and the audience an opportunity to distance themselves enough to see things from a different perspective - the past becomes history and thus gains the status of a parable: '[w]ith the past I find myself before a finished world, complete in all its elements, and I can thus more easily recompound it in my imagination. Here, no temptation for me to fall back to realism, nor for my readers to look for it' (Thurman, 1982: 264). Tellingly, Hannah Arendt in *Men in Dark Times* (1968) refers to Isak Dinesen in order to explain the social importance of the storyteller in society. According to Arendt, the storyteller is indeed the bearer of the values and meaning that regulate society, and he transmits them to his people by telling stories of universal understanding. As mentioned in the above quote from *Shadows in the Grass*, Blixen was led to write *Gengældelsens Veje* by the historical circumstances that surrounded her. In a difficult historical moment, it is consequently necessary to reconsider society and its values; the solution proposed by Blixen's works was to look at a different time, an idealised past, in order to enlighten a dark present. The past she chose is the one she termed 'gothic'. As Thurman explains, in Karen Blixen's art philosophy, gothic refers to the period that began in 1781 with the death of the Danish poet Johannes Ewald and ended in 1871 with the Second Empire. The Blixenian gothic was a period she saw as characterized by strong passions and people brave enough to live them. The symbol of such an ideal past was Lord Byron. Significantly in *Gengældelsens Veje*, Lucan's prince charming, Noel, is 'the very picture of Lord Byron' (Andrézel, 1947: 127). However distant Karen Blixen felt this work to be in relation to her other books, there is striking evidence that during her explorations in the unusual territory of the novel, she stayed loyal to her storyteller role. Despite the new authorial mask, it is still Isak Dinesen's storytelling technique that underpins Pierre Andrézel's narrative, as can be noted from the slightly fragmented structure of the novel. Furthermore, throughout the novel, tales are used with the storyteller's aim of making hard times more bearable and understandable. 'I shall tell you a story' is a recurrent formula in the novel that introduces us to the explanation of the most complex part of the story or to the way in which characters explain their feelings. That is the case in one of the last sections of the book, when – before going to face the evil Reverend – Zosine explains to Lucan the difference between bourgeois and aristocratic bravery, in order to encourage her to fight back.

On Africa, writing, and becoming Isak Dinesen

The definition Karen Blixen eventually gave to *Gengældelsens Veje* – as her 'life-saving book' (Dinesen, 1961: 132) – leads us to reflect on the inner meaning that writing meant to her. Fittingly, some critics, such as Clara Mucci, have defined Blixen's writing as 'exile narrative', where the exile experience is a rather peculiar one (2007). Her exile narrative, indeed, started in the very moment in which she went back to her mother land, Denmark, exiled from what she had always considered as her 'heart land', Africa. It is thus an inverse exile process. A stranger in her own country, amongst a culture and a mentality which she had tried so hard to distance herself from, she found herself needing to not only readapt, but also to build a new life. When asked about her choice of becoming a writer, she often remarked how accidental her decision had been: 'I shall always remain an amateur as a writer. Had I been able to keep my farm, I should never have written any books at all' (Hansen, 2003: 128). The loss of the farm and the death of her lover Denys Finch-Hatton were the tragedies that motivated her homecoming from Africa. It is revealing that her professional writing career started in her late forties, once she left what she later reckoned as her real life. Africa was the pivotal experience of her life, and the place through which she had the opportunity and the freedom to become who she wanted to be, a rare and precious experience for a woman of her time. Far away from the bourgeois and Victorian surroundings of her Danish family, she was finally able to shape her own identity. Geographical displacement thus acquires a fundamental function in the process that led to the creation of Karen Blixen's individuality, but also represents the first step towards becoming Isak Dinesen, the immortal storyteller. In Africa, she could not write about life, since she was too busy living it. Once back in Denmark, she devoted herself to writing, for economic purposes, but also because writing became her answer and reaction to the unbearable loss of Africa and Denys. She wrote in *Shadows on the Grass* that once back in Denmark she had great difficulty distinguishing reality from dream life, in which she was haunted by the vision of her beloved African landscape. In Denmark, she felt like the most important part of her life was over.

Literature and encouragement

In *Out of Africa*, Karen Blixen writes that writing became her refuge in the most critical period of crisis at the farm. Searching for a safe haven in the world of imagination was thus a practice she had already experimented with. Once back in Denmark, however, it became a strategy of survival. If the reality that surrounded her was difficult to grasp as authentic, the only thing left to make her feel alive was to create a parallel universe of tales closer to her most authentic part of life. Writing was mourning for a loss, but also the need to remember and to render universal and unforgettable the most intense years of her life. With *Gengældelsens Veje* Blixen shared this survival strategy with her readership, her fellow Danes, in one of the most difficult historical periods they had ever lived through. By providing them with the allegoric story of two innocent young girls who decide to resist and fight back against their oppressor, set in the period she considered the model of ideal bravery, she encouraged her troubled and tried audience not to give up.

Gengældelsens Veje can thus be seen as an attempt to fulfill the communication gap Blixen felt characterised her relationship with her countrymen. By deciding to write Seven Gothic Tales in English, she had erected an unequivocal wall between her and her homeland at the start of her writing career. Choosing a foreign language instead of one's mother tongue is certainly not a new phenomenon in literature, especially when it comes to authors who have been through an exile experience, or left their mother country. However, choosing a foreign language in one's own country, that is quite a different story. For Karen Blixen, choosing English represented an act of resistance, an attempt not to succumb to a culture into which she had never felt she fitted. But also, it was an act of affirmation of the identity she had worked so hard to shape during her African years. English was the language she spoke in Africa and represented for her the language of freedom. As a matter of fact, Blixen never felt understood by the Danish readership, stating:

> There is something in the Danish mentality I can't 'take', and I have felt myself lonely since I came home from Africa. The Danes speak all time of their sense of humor, 'det danske lune' but...they have so many times insisted upon taking me seriously, they have not been willing to play with me...It is a terribly disconcerting feeling to be the only intoxicated one at a party of very sober people, one feels oppressed. (Thurman, 1982: 307)

She felt that in the Anglo American literary world her art was better accepted and understood. Unsurprisingly, she was first published in the United States and the United Kingdom, by Random House, in 1934. When her first book was published in Denmark, in 1935, she predicted that the Danish audience would have difficulties in understanding it, stating 'I still believe that the Danish readership, which has not the slightest tradition for this kind of fantastical,- or nonsense,- type of literature, will ask, with some indignation: what is this all about?' (Hansen, 2003:14). Exile, or rather a feeling of ideological and geographical displacement, was her constant shadow after her return to Denmark. While Africa had represented the land of freedom, where freedom mainly consisted in the freedom of being oneself, the homecoming to Denmark was made even harder by what she felt to be a huge lack of communication with her own people. In becoming Isak Dinesen, Karen Blixen had to put Denmark aside. But with *Gengældelsens Veje*, under the tragic historical circumstances, she had to face her Danish audience, and understand their needs in such a peculiar historical moment. What the storyteller did, under the new novelistic mask of Pierre Andrézel, was to try to fill the communication gap with her countrymen, even if this would have run the risk of writing in her mother tongue and thus losing the protective distancing technique English provided. In *Gengældelsens Veje*, the feeling of geographical displacement, which characterises the rest of her production, becomes a feeling of linguistic displacement, a departure from the language in which she had constructed her writing career, but also the language that defined her identity as an author. With Pierre Andrézel, Blixen shared with her audience her own survival strategy, namely to tell a story that could fulfill a mutual need for escape. This unusual way of working also brought some advantages. Indeed, protected by the new pseudonym, she could experiment with a new register and a new way of writing. So Pierre Andrézel could, for example, feel free to coquettishly write: '[a] ball to a young girl is not only an experience or an adventure; it is a revelation. When she dances, she realizes why she exists, and why she was born' (1947: 40), or to digress on the prettiness of a new frock stating: '[i]t was made of heavy, very pale rose satin, with broad lace round the shoulders and the flounces, and to make the whole thing perfect, it was trimmed with buds of moss-roses, as live and fresh as if they had just been picked in the garden' (ibid. 37). Isak Dinesen would have never spent so much time on women's clothes. Free from the artistic responsibilities carried by her other famous pen name, in *Gengældelsens Veje*, Blixen found another voice, more playful and, perhaps, a little frivolous.

Conclusion

Gengældelsens Veje is an allegoric parable of resistance. As Karen Blixen herself noted in *Shadows on the Grass*, its happy ending was influenced by the success obtained by the Danish resistance movement in the last two years of occupation. Because of the book's inextricable connections to the historical context that surrounded Blixen, it is probably the closest one to her contemporaries she ever wrote. The storyteller's distancing strategy of setting the tale in the past served the purpose of giving the story a glow of authority, by rendering it a parable. The choice of writing it in Danish is deeply connected by her need to feel closer to her countrymen in an extremely difficult time, by writing something exclusively for them. *Gengældelsens Veje* raises the question of what kind of literature people need in time of crisis. The storyteller's answer is that they need to be entertained and distracted.

Blixen thus provided Danes with escape, entertainment and catharsis. A good storyteller, as Walter Benjamin writes in his essay 'The storyteller', will always be rooted in its people, and thus sense what kind of story they need (Benjamin, 1973: 100). A population under foreign occupation will need to be reminded that courage and heroes do exist. Even better, that common people can act heroically. *Gengældelsens Veje* fulfilled both these fundamental functions. The principal characters, Zosine and Lucan have no traits that would mark them as heroines. They are young, naïve, out of place in a society that required women to stay within the well-defined roles of mother, daughter or wife in order to be accepted. They have nothing in their favour, no predisposition to win. Yet, despite their position, they choose to stay, resist, and fight. And eventually, they win. But before the final victory, they have to face the abyss of the human psyche, the boundless evil of Reverend Pennhallow. As in a Greek tragedy, the final catharsis is gained only through suffering. The role of the storyteller is that of reminding society of the unchangeable laws and truths that regulate it, by presenting archetypical situations that can explain what would otherwise appear as inexplicable. A storyteller has, thus, a fundamental role in society, particularly in a society that has lost its sense of direction. The Danish scholar Hans Brix ends his analysis of the book by writing that at the end of the novel:

> Læserne lever op igen i sin egen fredelige stol i sin egen hyggelige stue. Hans hår falder til hvile.
>
> The reader comes back to his peaceful armchair in his cosy living room. His hair is no longer standing on end. (Brix, 1949: 235, my translation)

Since the time of the Greek tragedies, the function of intense stories has been to provide the reader with a deep experience of purification through catharsis. *Gengældelsens Veje* offered its contemporaries an experience of this kind. The reader is dragged through the horrors of the novel, forgetful of his or her own problems, yet getting closer to his deepest feelings and emotions, with the results of coming back to his life regenerated and, possibly, inspired. Here lies the salvational power of literature in time of crisis. What Karen Blixen tried to do with her unusual novel was to stimulate a reaction. However, since the circumstances obviously did not permit a clear and direct message, she expressed her truth the way she knew best – by telling a story.

Works cited

Andrézel, *Pierre. Gengældenlsens veje*. Copenaghen: Gyldendalske Boghandel Nordiske Forlag, 1944.

---. *The Angelic Avengers*. New York: Random House, 1947.

Dinesen, Isak. *Out of Africa*. London: Putnam, 1937.

---. *Daguerreotypes and Other Essays*. Chicago: The University of Chicago Press, 1979.

---. *Shadows on the Grass*. New York: Random House, 1961.

---. *Last Tales*. London: Putnam, 1957.

Arendt, Hannah. *Men in dark times*. New York: Harcourt, Brace and World, 1968.

Benjamin, Walter. *Illuminations*, edited by Hannah Arendt. London: Fontana, 1973

Brix, Hans. *Karen Blixens eventyr*. Copenhagen: Gyldendalske Boghandel Nordiske Forlag, 1949.

Hale, Dorothy J. *The Novel, an anthology of criticism and theory, 1900-2000*. Malden, Mass., Oxford: Blackwell Publishing, 2006.

Hannah, Donald. *Isak Dinensen and Karen Blixen, the mask and the reality*. London: Putnam, 1971.

Hansen, Leander Frantz. *The Aristocratic Universe of Karen Blixen*. Brighton: Sussex Academic Press, 2003.

Langbaum, Robert. *Isak Dinesen's Art: The Gayety of vision*. Chicago: University of Chicago Press, 1975.

Lasson, Frans. *Letters from Africa, 1914-1931 / Isak Dinesen*. Chicago:

University of Chicago Press, 1981.

Mucci, Clara. *Tempeste, Narrazione di esilio in Shakespeare e Karen Blixen.* Naples: Liguori Press, 2007.

Thurman, Judith. *Isak Dinensen: The Life of Karen Blixen.* London: Weidenfeld and Nicolson, 1982.

Wilkinson, Lynn R. 'Hannah Arendt on Isak Dinesen: Between storytelling and theory.' *Comparative Literature* 56.1, 2004, 77-98.

www.ingramcontent.com/pod-product-compliance
Lightning Source LLC
Chambersburg PA
CBHW060348190426
43201CB00043B/1771